Dinah Zike's
High School American History Reading and Study Skills

FOLDABLES™

McGraw Hill Glencoe

New York, New York   Columbus, Ohio   Chicago, Illinois   Peoria, Illinois   Woodland Hills, California

The McGraw-Hill Companies

Send all inquiries to:
Glencoe/McGraw-Hill
8787 Orion Place
Columbus, OH 43240-4027

ISBN 0-07-860518-0

Printed in the United States of America

4 5 6 7 8 9 10   024   08 07 06 05

Table of Contents

Introduction to Foldables

Folding Instructions

Topic-Specific Foldables 43

Dear Teacher,

What is a Foldable?

A Foldable is a 3-D, student-made, interactive graphic organizer based upon a skill. Making a Foldable gives students a fast, kinesthetic activity that helps them organize and retain information. Each unit in the student edition of the textbook begins with a Foldable that can be used as a Study Organizer. Each unit's Foldable is designed to be used as a study guide for the main ideas and key points presented in the unit. Foldables can also be used for a more in-depth investigation of a concept, idea, opinion, event, or a person or place studied in a unit. The purpose of this ancillary is to show you how to create various types of Foldables and provide chapter-specific Foldables examples. With this information, you can individualize Foldables to meet your curriculum needs.

This book is divided into two sections. The first section presents step-by-step instructions, illustrations, and photographs of 34 Foldables, many of which were not used in the student edition. I've included over 100 photographs to help you visualize ways in which they might enhance instruction. The second section presents additional Foldables activities for each chapter in the textbook. I highly suggest making this book available as a source for students who wish to learn new and creative ways in which to make study guides, present projects, or do extra credit work.

Who Am I?

You may have seen Foldables featured in this book used in supplemental programs or staff-development workshops. Today my Foldables are used internationally. I present workshops and keynote addresses to over fifty thousand teachers and parents a year, sharing Foldables that I began inventing, designing, and adapting over thirty five years ago. Students of all ages are using them for daily work, note-taking activities, student-directed projects, forms of alternative assessment, journals, graphs, tables, and more.

Have fun using and adapting Foldables,

Dinah Zike

Why use Foldables in Social Studies?

When teachers ask me why they should take time to use the Foldables featured in this book, I explain that they:

- quickly organize, display, and arrange data, making it easier for students to grasp social studies concepts, theories, facts, opinions, questions, research, and ideas. They also help sequence events as outlined in the content standards.

- result in student-made study guides that are compiled as students listen for main ideas, read for main ideas, or conduct research.

- provide a multitude of creative formats in which students can present projects, research, interviews, and inquiry-based reports instead of typical poster board or social studies fair formats.

- replace teacher-generated writing or photocopied sheets with student-generated print.

- incorporate the use of such skills as comparing and contrasting, recognizing cause and effect, and finding similarities and differences into daily work and long-term projects. For example, these Foldables can be used to compare and contrast student explanations and/or opinions to explanations and/or opinions currently accepted by experts in the field of social studies.

- continue to "immerse" students in previously learned vocabulary, concepts, information, generalizations, ideas, and theories, providing them with a strong foundation that they can build upon with new observations, concepts, and knowledge.

- can be used by students or teachers to easily communicate data through graphs, tables, charts, models, and diagrams, including Venn diagrams.

- allow students to make their own journals for recording observations, research information, primary and secondary source data, surveys, and more.

- can be used as alternative assessment tools by teachers to evaluate student progress or by students to evaluate their own progress.

- integrate language arts, the sciences, and mathematics into the study of social studies.

- provide a sense of student ownership in the social studies curriculum.

Foldable Basics

What to Write and Where

Teach students to write general information such as titles, vocabulary words, concepts, questions, main ideas, and dates, on the front tabs of their Foldables. General information is viewed every time a student looks at a Foldable. Foldables help students focus on and remember key points without being distracted by other print.

Ask students to write specific information—supporting ideas, student thoughts, answers to questions, research information, empirical data, class notes, observations, and definitions—under the tabs.

As you teach, demonstrate different ways in which Foldables can be used. Soon you will find that students make their own Foldables and use them independently for study guides and projects.

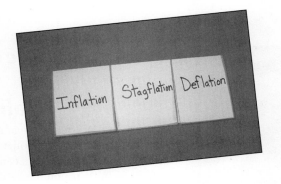
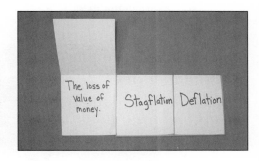

With or Without Tabs

Foldables with flaps or tabs create study guides that students can use to check what they know about the general information on the front of tabs. Use Foldables without tabs for assessment purposes or projects where information is presented for others to view quickly.

Venn Diagram used as a study guide

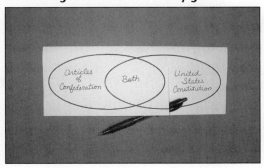

Venn Diagram used for assessment

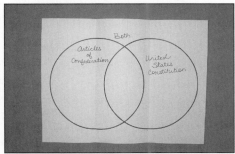

What to Do with Scissors and Glue

If it is difficult for your elementary students to keep glue and scissors at their desks, set up a small table in the classroom and provide several containers of glue, numerous pairs of scissors (sometimes tied to the table), containers of crayons and colored pencils, a stapler, clear tape, and anything else you think students might need to make their Foldables. Don't be surprised if students donate colored markers, decorative-edged scissors, gel pens, stencils, and other art items to your publishing table.

The more they make and use graphic organizers, the faster students become at producing them.

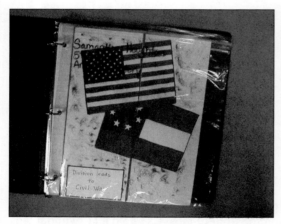

Storing Graphic Organizers in Student Portfolios

Turn one-gallon freezer bags into student portfolios which can be collected and stored in the classroom. Students can also carry their portfolios in their notebooks if they place strips of two-inch clear tape along one side and punch three holes through the taped edge.

Have each student write his or her name along the top of the plastic portfolio with a permanent marker and cover the writing with two-inch clear tape to keep it from wearing off.

Cut the bottom corners off the bag so it won't hold air and will stack and store easily.

HINT: *I found it more convenient to keep student portfolios in my classroom so student work was always available when needed and not "left at home" or "in the car." Giant laundry-soap boxes make good storage containers for portfolios.*

Let Students Use This Book As an Idea Reference

Make this book of lists available to students to use as an idea reference for projects, discussions, social studies debates, extra credit work, cooperative learning group presentations, and more.

Using Visuals and Graphics with Foldables

I designed the graphics on pages 8–11 to be used as visual aids for student production, while immersing students in measurement, percentages, maps, and time lines. At times, I require these graphics to be used in student presentations. I photocopy them or print them from my computer and pass them out. At other times, students incorporate them into their journals, notes, projects, and study guides independently. I found that students and teachers were more likely to use graphics if they were available on a classroom computer where they could be selected and printed out as needed.

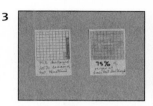

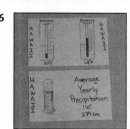

1. Mark and label large United States and world maps to show where past and recent events occurred, where a historic person lived and worked, where wars were fought and battles won, where volcanoes are active and inactive, where boundaries of territories or regions existed, etc.

2. Mark and label smaller maps of continents to illustrate more specific locations, for example, when making a "who, what, when, where" Foldable.

3. Hundreds grids can be used to illustrate percentages, decimals, and bar graphs.

4. Use time lines to record when someone lived or when an event or sequence of events occurred. Use two parallel time lines to compare what was happening in two different areas at the same time.

5. Use small picture frames to sketch or name a person, place, or thing. Great to use with the four-door book as a "who, what, when, where" activity.

6. Use rain gauges and thermometers in projects to record average precipitation amounts or average seasonal temperatures of a geographic area.

> **NOTE:** *I grant you permission to photocopy these pages and place copies of them in the production center or publishing center of your classroom. I also grant you permission to scan these pages and use them electronically.*

National Social Studies Standards and Communication Skills

The National Social Studies Standards stress the importance of communication skills in social studies education. Not all students will become government officials, geographers, or historians, but all students need to be able to think, analyze, and communicate using social studies skills. Throughout their lives, students will be called upon to be literate in social studies as they make observations, analyze and recall empirical data, read and differentiate between fact and opinion, discuss pros and cons of actions and reactions, justify voting for or against an issue, research a topic related to their well-being or interests, make cause-and-effect decisions about their actions, write letters to the editor to express their views publicly, and more. Foldables are one of many techniques that can be used to integrate reading, writing, thinking, debating, researching, and other communication skills into an interdisciplinary social studies curriculum.

Basic Foldable Shapes

The following figures illustrate the basic folds that are referred to throughout the following section of this book.

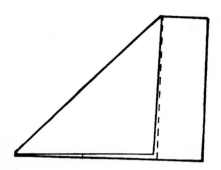

Taco Fold

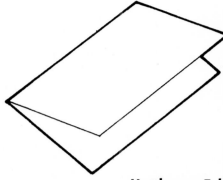

Hamburger Fold

Hot Dog Fold

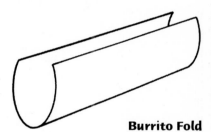

Burrito Fold

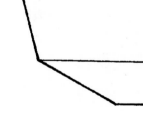

Valley Fold

Shutter Fold

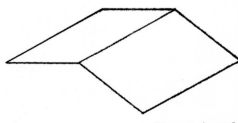

Mountain Fold

Half-Book

Fold a sheet of paper (8 1/2" x 11") in half.

1. This book can be folded vertically like a *hot dog* or . . .

2. . . . it can be folded horizontally like a *hamburger*.

Use this book for descriptive, expository, persuasive, or narrative writing, as well as for graphs, diagrams, or charts.

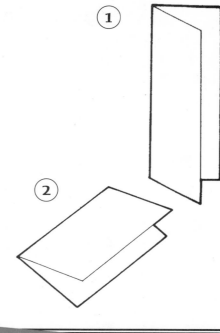

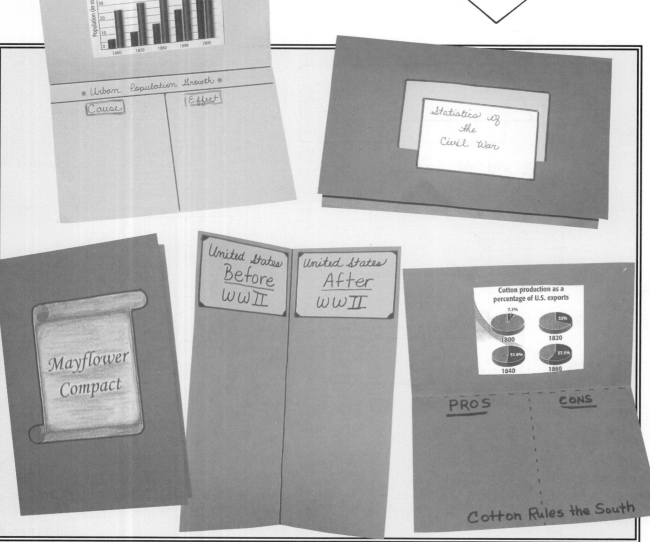

Folded Book

1. Make a *half-book*.

2. Fold it in half again like a *hamburger*. This produces a ready-made cover, and two small pages for information on the inside.

Use photocopied work sheets, Internet printouts, and student-drawn diagrams or maps to create this book. One sheet of paper becomes two activities and two grades.

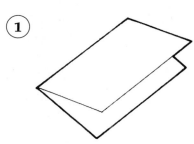

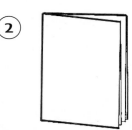

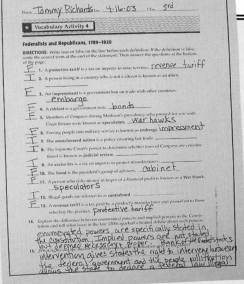

When folded, the worksheet becomes a book for recording notes and questions.

Three-Quarter Book

1. Take a *two-tab* book and raise the left-hand tab.

2. Cut the tab off at the top fold line.

3. A larger book of information can be made by gluing several *three-quarter books* side-by-side.

Sketch or glue a graphic to the left, write one or more questions on the right, and record answers and information under the right tab.

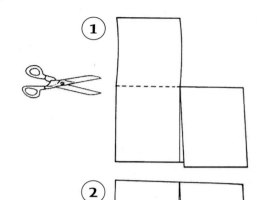

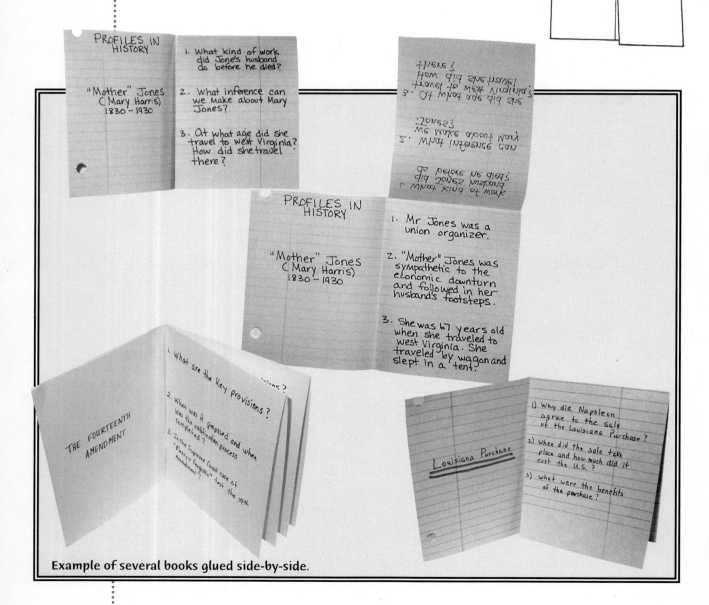

Example of several books glued side-by-side.

Bound Book

1. Take two sheets of paper (8 1/2" x 11") and separately fold them like a *hamburger*. Place the papers on top of each other, leaving one-sixteenth of an inch between the *mountain tops*.

2. Mark both folds one inch from the outer edges.

3. On one of the folded sheets, cut from the top and bottom edge to the marked spot on both sides.

4. On the second folded sheet, start at one of the marked spots and cut the fold between the two marks.

5. Take the cut sheet from step 3 and fold it like a *burrito*. Place the *burrito* through the other sheet and then open the *burrito*. Fold the bound pages in half to form an eight-page book.

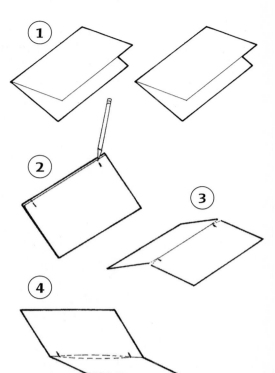

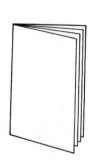

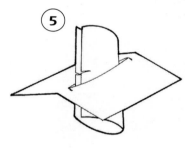

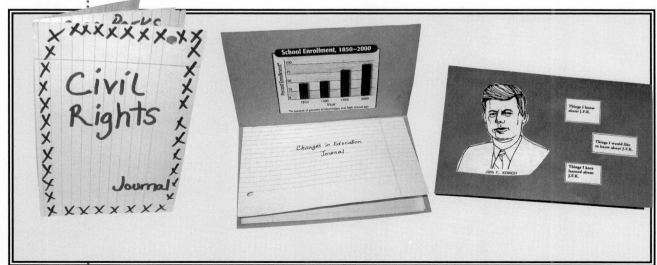

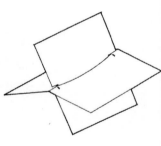

Two-Tab Book

1. Take a *folded book* and cut up the *valley* of the inside fold toward the *mountain top*. This cut forms two large tabs that can be used front and back for writing and illustrations.

2. The book can be expanded by making several of these folds and gluing them side-by-side.

Use this book with data occurring in twos. For example, use it for comparing and contrasting, determining cause and effect, finding similarities and differences, and more.

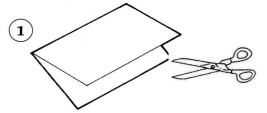

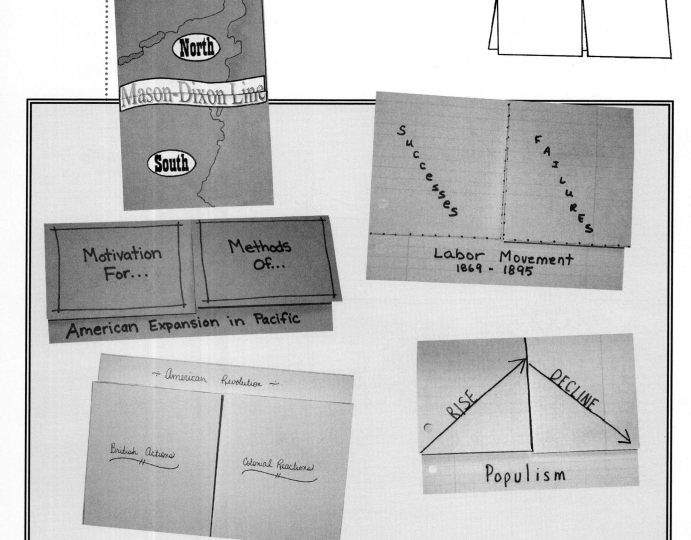

Pocket Book

1. Fold a sheet of paper (8 1/2" x 11") in half like a *hamburger*.

2. Open the folded paper and fold one of the long sides up two inches to form a pocket. Refold along the *hamburger* fold so that the newly formed pockets are on the inside.

3. Glue the outer edges of the two-inch fold with a small amount of glue.

4. **Optional:** Glue a cover around the *pocket book*.

   Variation: Make a multi-paged booklet by gluing several pockets side-by-side. Glue a cover around the multi-paged *pocket book*.

Use 3" x 5" index cards inside the pockets. Store student-made books, such as two-tab books and folded books in the pockets.

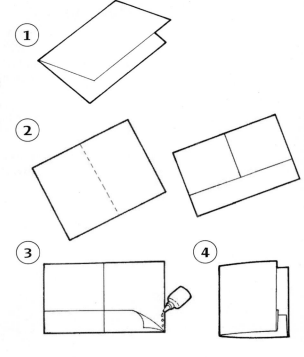

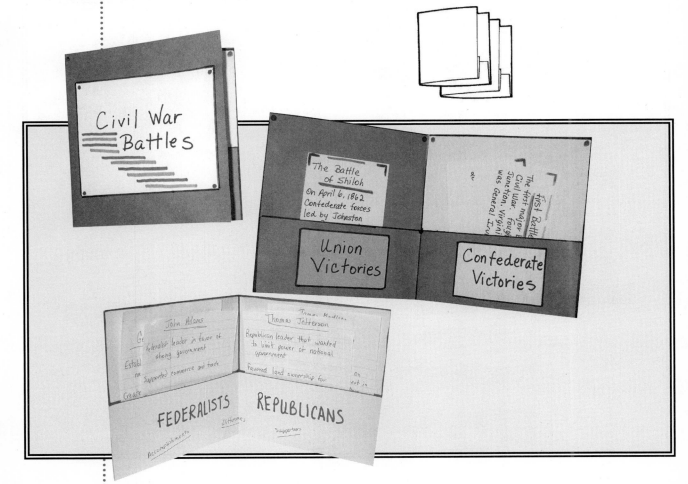

Matchbook

1. Fold a sheet of paper (8 1/2" x 11") like a *hamburger,* but fold it so that one side is one inch longer than the other side.

2. Fold the one-inch tab over the short side forming an envelope-like fold.

3. Cut the front flap in half toward the *mountain top* to create two flaps.

Use this book to report on one thing, such as one person, place, or thing, or for reporting on two things, such as the cause and effect of Western expansion.

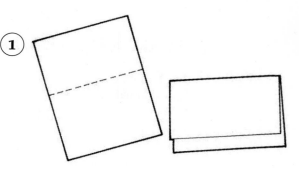

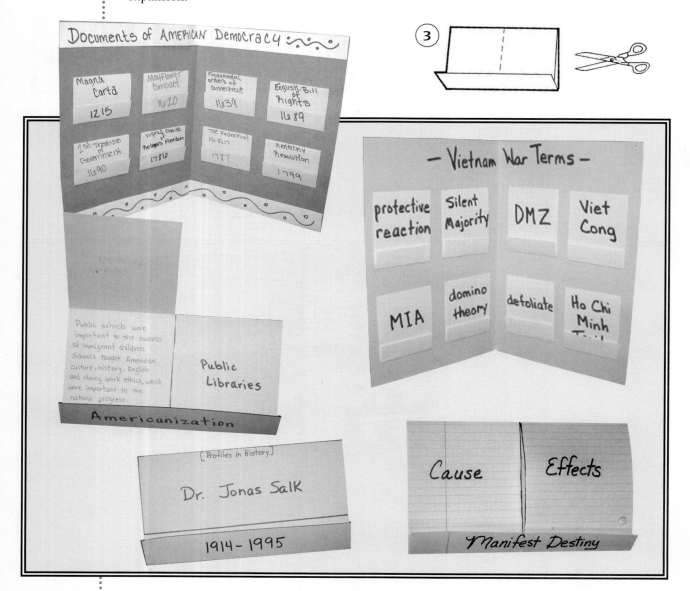

Shutter Fold

1. Begin as if you were going to make a *hamburger* but instead of creasing the paper, pinch it to show the midpoint.

2. Fold the outer edges of the paper to meet at the pinch, or mid-point, forming a *shutter fold*.

Use this book for data occurring in twos. Or, make this fold using 11" x 17" paper and smaller books—such as the half book, journal, and two-tab book—that can be glued inside to create a large project full of student work.

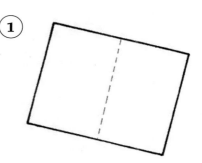

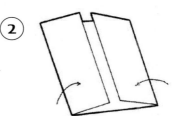

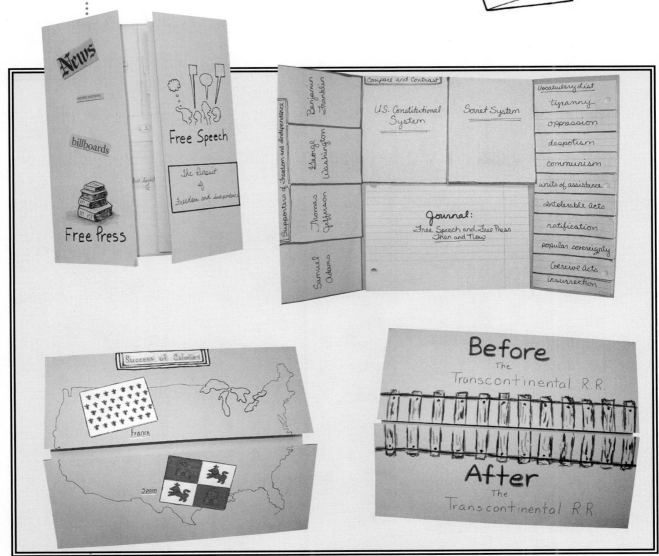

Trifold Book

1. Fold a sheet of paper (8 1/2" x 11") into thirds.

2. Use this book as is, or cut into shapes. If the trifold is cut, leave plenty of fold on both sides of the designed shape, so the book will open and close in three sections.

Use this book to make charts with three columns or rows, large Venn diagrams, reports on data occurring in threes, or to show the outside and inside of something and to write about it.

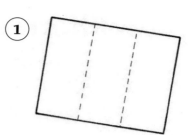

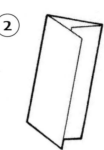

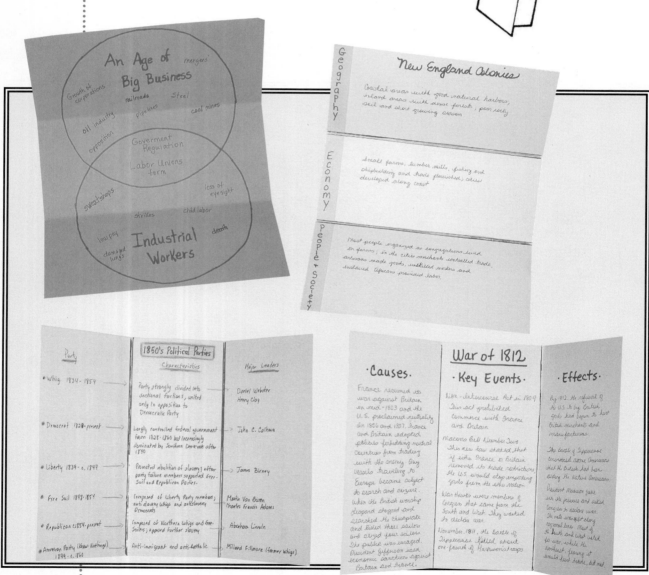

Three-Tab Book

1. Fold a sheet of paper like a *hot dog*.

2. With the paper horizontal, and the fold of the *hot dog* up, fold the right side toward the center, trying to cover one half of the paper.

NOTE: *If you fold the right edge over first, the final graphic organizer will open and close like a book.*

3. Fold the left side over the right side to make a book with three folds.

4. Open the folded book. Place your hands between the two thicknesses of paper and cut up the two *valleys* on one side only. This will form three tabs.

Use this book for data occurring in threes, and for two-part Venn diagrams.

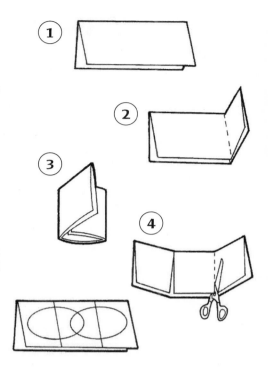

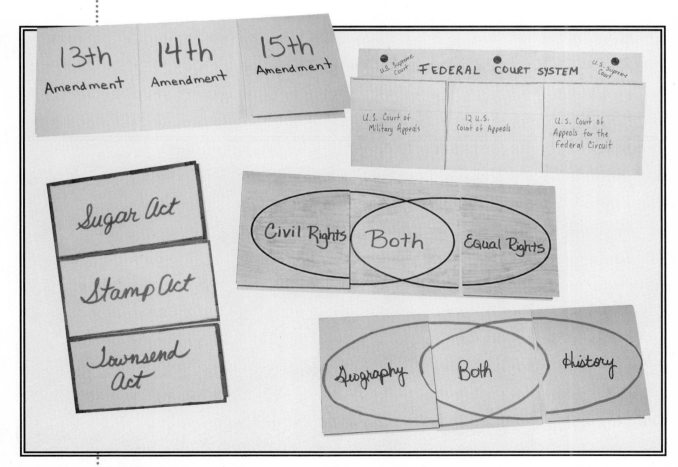

Pyramid Fold

1. Fold a sheet of paper (8 1/2" x 11") into a *taco*, forming a square. Cut off the excess rectangular tab formed by the fold.

2. Open the folded *taco* and refold it the opposite way forming another *taco* and an X-fold pattern.

3. Cut one of the folds to the center of the X, or the midpoint, and stop. This forms two triangular-shaped flaps.

4. Glue one of the flaps under the other, forming a *pyramid*.

5. Label front sections and write information, notes, thoughts, and questions inside the pyramid on the back of the appropriate tab.

Use to make mobiles and dioramas. Use with data occurring in threes.

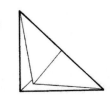

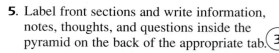

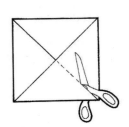

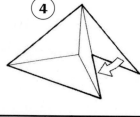

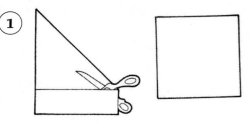

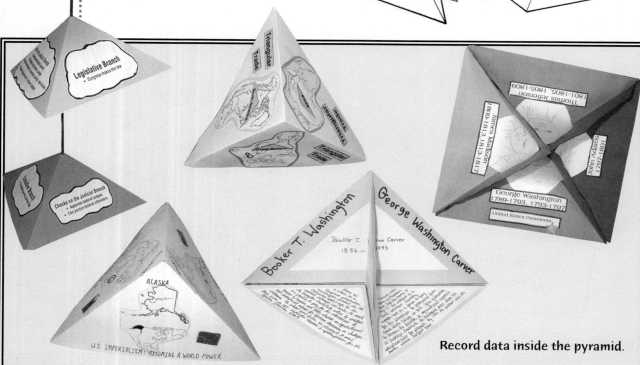

Record data inside the pyramid.

Layered-Look Book

1. Stack two sheets of paper (8 1/2" x 11") so that the back sheet is one inch higher than the front sheet.

2. Bring the bottom of both sheets upward and align the edges so that all of the layers or tabs are the same distance apart.

3. When all tabs are an equal distance apart, fold the papers and crease well.

4. Open the papers and glue them together along the *valley* or inner center fold or, staple them along the *mountain*.

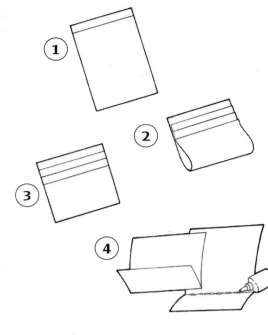

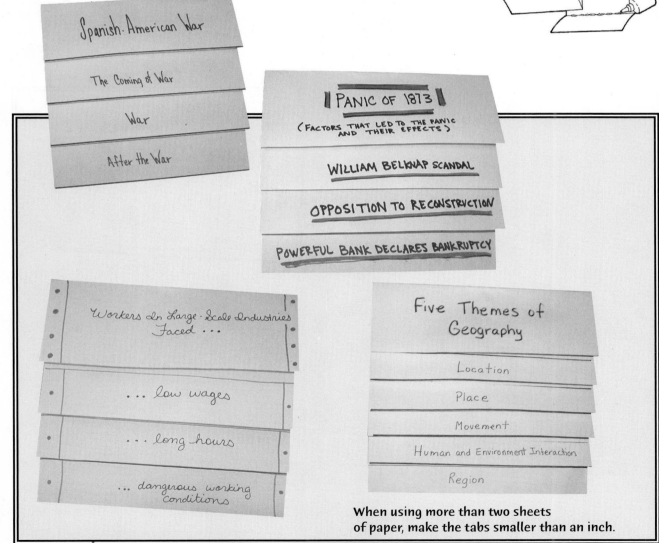

Spanish-American War

The Coming of War

War

After the War

PANIC OF 1873
(FACTORS THAT LED TO THE PANIC AND THEIR EFFECTS)

WILLIAM BELKNAP SCANDAL

OPPOSITION TO RECONSTRUCTION

POWERFUL BANK DECLARES BANKRUPTCY

Workers In Large-Scale Industries Faced ...

... low wages

... long hours

... dangerous working conditions

Five Themes of Geography

Location

Place

Movement

Human and Environment Interaction

Region

When using more than two sheets of paper, make the tabs smaller than an inch.

Four-Tab Book

1. Fold a sheet of paper (8 1/2" x 11") in half like a *hot dog*.

2. Fold this long rectangle in half like a *hamburger*.

3. Fold both ends back to touch the *mountain top* or fold it like an *accordion*.

4. On the side with two *valleys* and one *mountain top,* make vertical cuts through one thickness of paper, forming four tabs.

Use this book for data occurring in fours. For example: community, city, state, and nation.

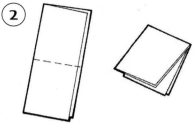
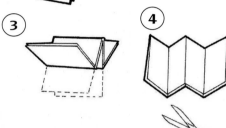

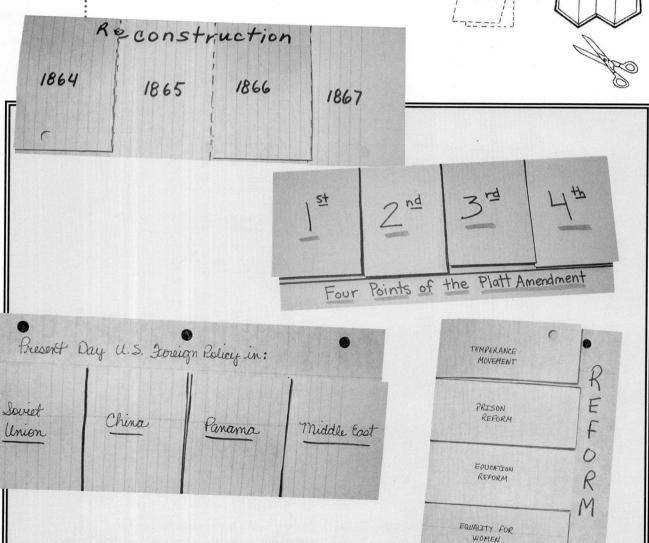

Reconstruction

1864   1865   1866   1867

1st   2nd   3rd   4th

Four Points of the Platt Amendment

Present Day U.S. Foreign Policy in:

Soviet Union   China   Panama   Middle East

TEMPERANCE MOVEMENT

PRISON REFORM

EDUCATION REFORM

EQUALITY FOR WOMEN

R E F O R M

Standing Cube

1. Use two sheets of the same size paper. Fold each like a *hamburger,* but, fold one side one half inch shorter than the other. This will make a tab that extends out one half inch on one side.

2. Fold the long side over the short side of both sheets of paper, making tabs.

3. On one of the folded papers, place a small amount of glue along the the small folded tab, next to the *valley* but not in it.

4. Place the non-folded edge of the second sheet of paper square into the *valley* and fold the glue-covered tab over this sheet of paper. Press flat until the glue holds. Repeat with the other side.

5. Allow the glue to dry completely before continuing. After the glue has dried, the cube can be collapsed flat to allow students to work at their desks. The cube can also be folded into fourths for easier storage, or for moving it to a display area.

Use with data occurring in fours or make it into a project. Make a small display cube using 8 1/2" x 11" paper. Use 11" x 17" paper to make large project cubes that you can glue other books onto for display. Notebook paper, photocopied sheets, magazine pictures, and current events also can be displayed on the large cube.

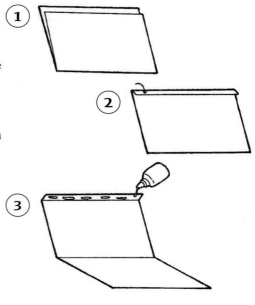
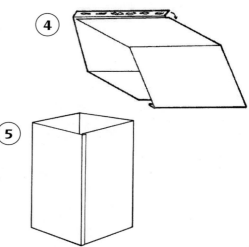

This large cube project can be stored in plastic bag portfolios.

Envelope Fold

1. Fold a sheet of paper (8 1/2" x 11") into a *taco* forming a square. Cut off the excess paper strip formed by the square.

2. Open the folded *taco* and refold it the opposite way forming another *taco* and an X fold pattern.

3. Open the *taco* fold and fold the corners toward the center point of the X forming a small square.

4. Trace this square on another sheet of paper. Cut and glue it to the inside of the envelope. Pictures can be placed under or on top of the tabs, or can be used to teach fractional parts.

Use this book for data occurring in fours. For example: North, South, East, and West

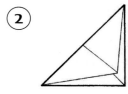

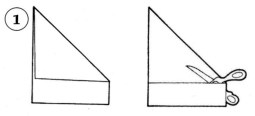

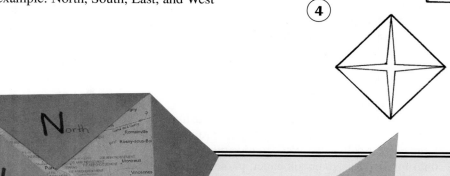

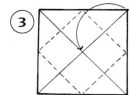

Four-Door Book

1. Make a *shutter fold* using 11" x 17" or 12" x 18" paper.

2. Fold the *shutter fold* in half like a *hamburger.* Crease well.

3. Open the project and cut along the two inside *valley* folds.

4. These cuts will form four doors on the inside of the project.

Use this fold for data occurring in fours. When folded in half like a *hamburger,* a finished *four-door book* can be glued inside a large (11" x 17") *shutter fold* as part of a larger project.

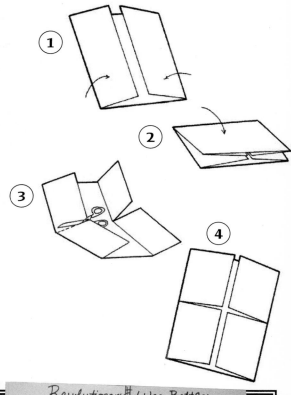

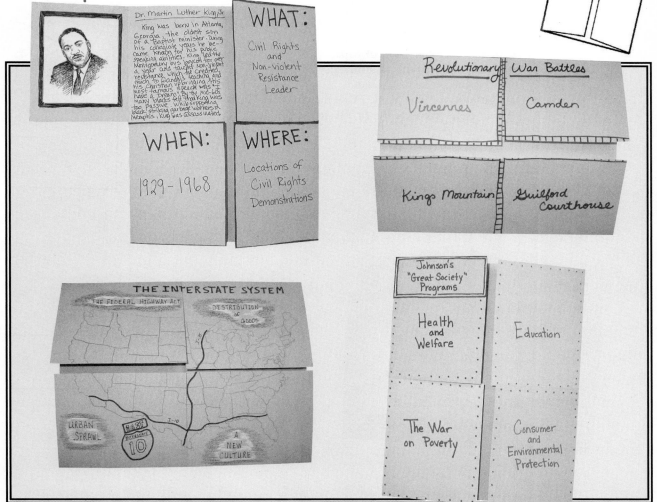

Top-Tab Book

1. Fold a sheet of paper (8 1/2" x 11") in half like a *hamburger*. Cut the center fold, forming two half sheets.

2. Fold one of the half sheets four times. Begin by folding in half like a *hamburger,* fold again like a *hamburger,* and finally again like a *hamburger.* This folding has formed your pattern of four rows and four columns, or 16 small squares.

3. Fold two sheets of paper (8 1/2" x 11") in half like a *hamburger.* Cut the center folds, forming four half sheets.

4. Hold the pattern vertically and place on a half sheet of paper under the pattern. Cut the bottom right hand square out of both sheets. Set this first page aside.

5. Take a second half sheet of paper and place it under the pattern. Cut the first and second right hand squares out of both sheets. Place the second page on top of the first page.

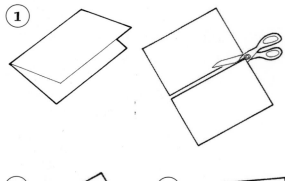

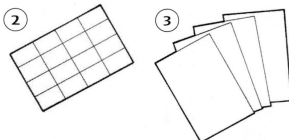

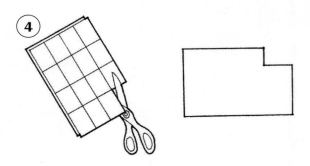

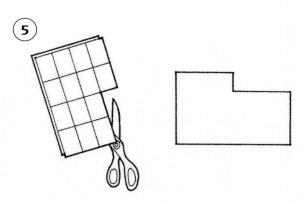

6. Take a third half sheet of paper and place it under the pattern. Cut the first, second, and third right hand squares out of both sheets. Place this third page on top of the second page.

7. Place the fourth, uncut half sheet of paper behind the three cut out sheets, leaving four aligned tabs across the top of the book. Staple several times on the left side. You can also place glue along the left paper edges, and stack them together. The glued spine is very strong.

8. Cut a final half sheet of paper with no tabs and staple along the left side to form a cover.

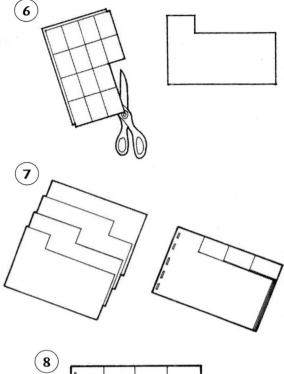

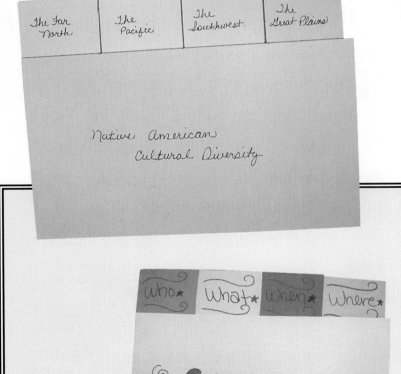

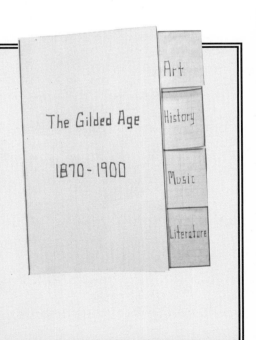

Accordion Book

NOTE: *Steps 1 and 2 should be done only if paper is too large to begin with.*

1. Fold the selected paper into *hamburgers.*

2. Cut the paper in half along the fold lines.

3. Fold each section of paper into *hamburgers,* but fold one side one half inch shorter than the other side. This will form a tab that is one half inch long.

4. Fold this tab forward over the shorter side, and then fold it back away from the shorter piece of paper; in other words, fold it the opposite way.

5. To form an *accordion,* glue a straight edge of one section into the *valley* of another section.

NOTE: *Stand the sections on end to form an* accordion *to help students visualize how to glue them together. (See illustration.)*

Always place the extra tab at the back of the book so you can add more pages later.

Use this book for time lines, student projects that grow, sequencing events or data, and biographies.

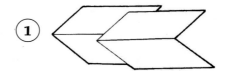
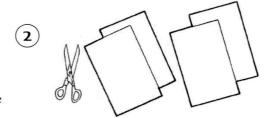
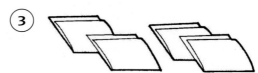
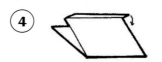
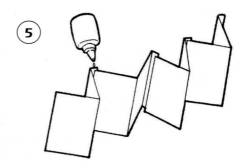

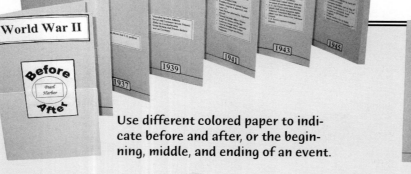

Use different colored paper to indicate before and after, or the beginning, middle, and ending of an event.

When folded, this project is used like a book, and it can be stored in student portfolios. When open, it makes a nice project display. Accordion books can be stored in file cabinets for future use, too.

Pop-Up Book

1. Fold a sheet of paper (8 1/2" x 11") in half like a *hamburger*.

2. Beginning at the fold, or *mountain* top, cut one or more tabs.

3. Fold the tabs back and forth several times until there is a good fold line formed.

4. Partially open the *hamburger* fold and push the tabs through to the inside.

5. With one small dot of glue, glue figures for the *pop-up book* to the front of each tab. Allow the glue to dry before going on to the next step.

6. Make a cover for the book by folding another sheet of paper in half like a *hamburger*. Place glue around the outside edges of the *pop-up book* and firmly press inside the *hamburger* cover.

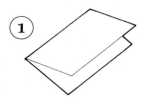

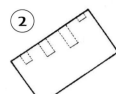

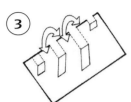

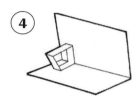

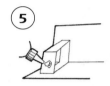

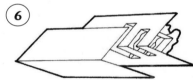

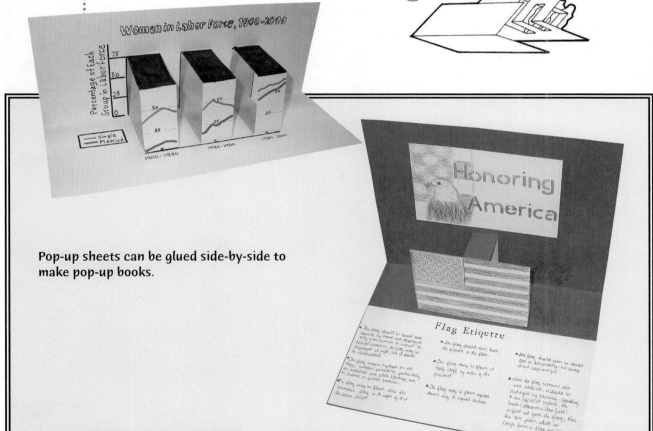

Pop-up sheets can be glued side-by-side to make pop-up books.

Five-Tab Book

1. Fold a sheet of paper in half like a *hot dog* or *hamburger* for a five tab book, or leave open for a folded table or chart.

2. Fold the paper so that one third is exposed and two thirds are covered.

3. Fold the two thirds section in half.

4. Fold the one third section (single thickness) backward to form a fold line.

The paper will be divided into fifths when opened

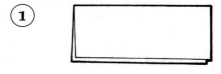

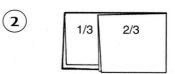

②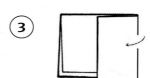

③

④

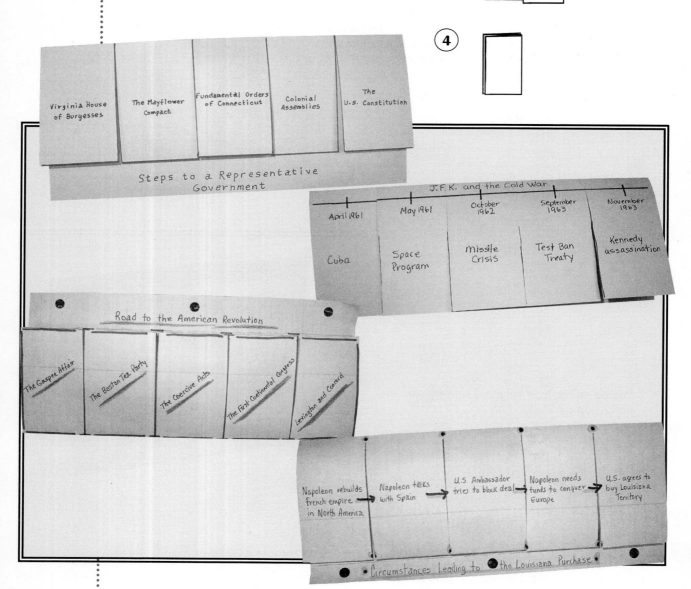

Folded Table or Chart

1. Fold the number of vertical columns needed to make the table or chart.

2. Fold the horizontal rows needed to make the table or chart.

3. Label the rows and columns.

Remember: Tables are organized along vertical and horizontal axes, while charts are organized along one axis, either horizontal or vertical.

Table

Chart

Compare	Federalists	Democratic-Republicans
Role of federal Government?	Strong central government	Limited federal government with emphasis on state's rights
Leaders	Hamilton	Jefferson
Supporters	artisans, bankers, merchants, urban workers, Eastern farmers, manufacturers	rural Southern and Western landowners

Explorer	Region	Date
Christopher Columbus	Caribbean Islands, Central American coast, N. South America	1492-1504
Amerigo Vespucci	N. South America, Caribbean Islands	1499-1500
Pedro Cabral	South America	1500
John Cabot	North America	1497-1498
Martin Frobisher	Between North America and Greenland	1576-1578
Giovanni da Verrazano	North America, Newfoundland	1524
Jacques Cartier	Newfoundland, North America	1534
Henry Hudson	Scandinavia, Newfoundland, North America	1609

Culture	Where did they live?	How did they live?
Hohokam	Desert of present-day Arizona in an area between the Gila and Salt River valleys.	Very resourceful in water management. Dug hundreds of miles of irrigation channels, pottery, carved stone, and etched shells.
Anasazi	In the area known as the four corners, the meeting place of Utah, Colorado, Arizona, and New Mexico.	Built pueblos and complex road systems. Also built cliff dwellings.
Mound Builders	Central North America between Pennsylvania and the Mississippi River Valley.	Built huge earth mounds in the shapes of pyramids or animals. Some mounds contained burial chambers.
Inuit	Northernmost part of North America around the Arctic circle.	Lived in igloos, wore furs and seal skins. Inuit were hunters and fishers and built skin covered boats.
Tlingit	Northwestern coast of North America.	Used resources of the forest and sea. Built wooden houses and canoes. Trapped and fished.

Folding a Circle Into Tenths

1. Fold a paper circle in half.

2. Fold the half circle so that one third is exposed and two thirds are covered.

3. Fold the one third (single thickness) backward to form a fold line.

4. Fold the two thirds section in half.

5. The half circle will be divided into fifths. When opened, the circle will be divided into tenths.

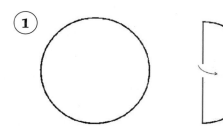

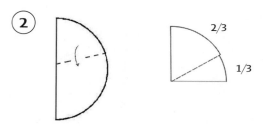

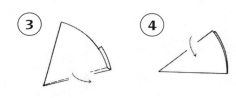

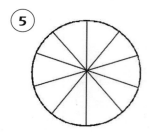

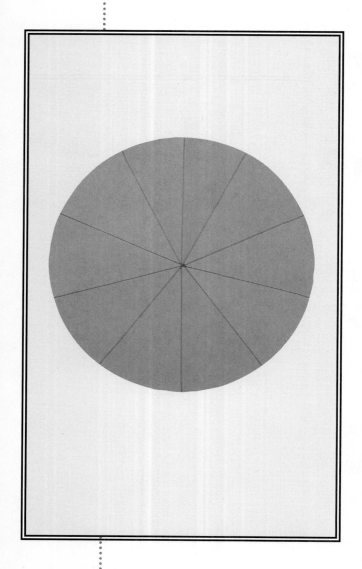

NOTE: *Paper squares and rectangles are folded into tenths the same way. Fold them so that one third is exposed and two thirds is covered. Continue with steps 3 and 4.*

Circle Graph

1. Cut out two circles using a pattern.

2. Fold one of the circles in half on each axis, forming fourths. Cut along one of the fold lines (the radius) to the middle of each circle. Flatten the circle.

3. Slip the two circles together along the cuts until they overlap completely.

4. Spin one of the circles while holding the other stationary. Estimate how much of each of the two (or you can add more) circles should be exposed to illustrate given percentages or fractional parts of data. Add circles to represent more than two percentages.

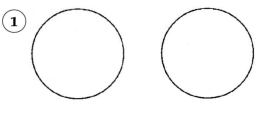

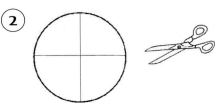

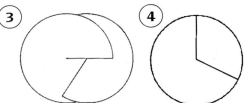

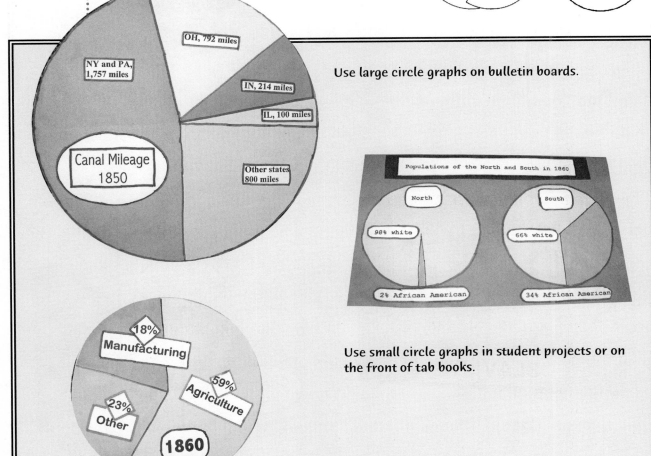

Use large circle graphs on bulletin boards.

Use small circle graphs in student projects or on the front of tab books.

Concept-Map Book

1. Fold a sheet of paper along the long or short axis, leaving a two-inch tab uncovered along the top.

2. Fold in half or in thirds.

3. Unfold and cut along the two or three inside fold lines.

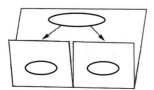

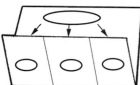

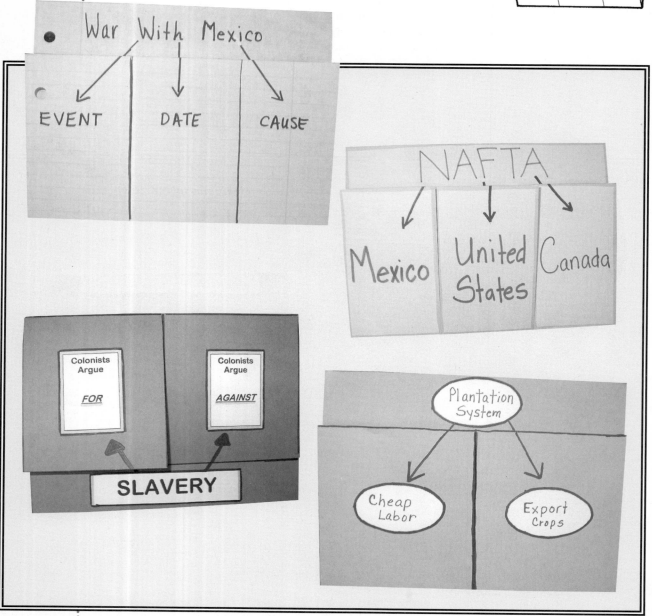

Vocabulary Book

1. Fold a sheet of notebook paper in half like a *hotdog*.

2. On one side, cut every third line. This results in ten tabs on wide ruled notebook paper and twelve tabs on college ruled.

3. Label the tabs.

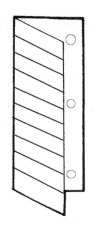

Use to take notes and record data. Leave the notebook holes uncovered and it can be stored in a notebook.

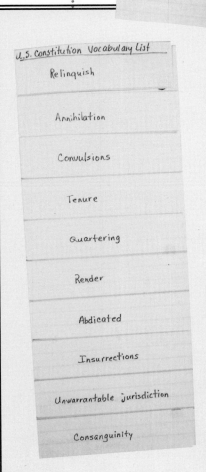

Amendments

Guarantees freedom of religion, speech, assembly, and press, and the right of the people to petition the government.

2
3
4
5
6
7
8
9
10

Bill of Rights

Questions and Answers

1. How did Microsoft differ from other computer companies?

2. How did deregulation affect the telecommunications industry?

3. How did the Internet expand business opportunities?

4. Why did President Clinton's proposed health care plan fail?

5. What two reforms did Clinton and Congress agree to support?

6. What events led to the impeachment of Clinton?

7. Why was the European Union (EU) created in 1993?

8. What was President G.W. Bush's first priority when he took office?

9. What are the three main reasons certain Muslims became angry with the U.S.?

10. How did Americans respond to the 9/11 attacks?

Use for recording student questions and answers.

U.S. Constitution Vocabulary List

Relinquish

Annihilation

Convulsions

Tenure

Quartering

Render

Abdicated

Insurrections

Unwarrantable jurisdiction

Consanguinity

Use for vocabulary books.

Four-Door Diorama

1. Make a *four-door book* out of a *shutter fold*.

2. Fold the two inside corners back to the outer edges (*mountains*) of the *shutter fold*. This will result in two *tacos* that will make the *four-door book* look like it has a shirt collar. Do the same thing to the bottom of the *four-door book*. When finished, four small triangular *tacos* have been made.

3. Form a 90-degree angle and overlap the folded triangles to make a display case that doesn't use staples or glue. (It can be collapsed for storage.)

4. Or, as illustrated, cut off all four triangles, or *tacos*. Staple or glue the sides.

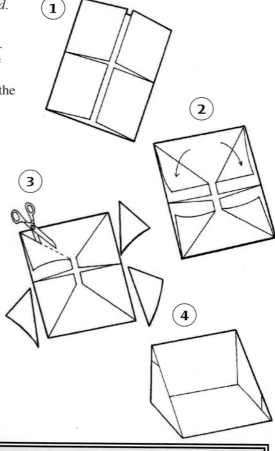

Use 11" x 17" paper to make a large display case.

Use poster board to make giant display cases.

Glue display cases end-to-end to compare and contrast or to sequence events or data.

Picture-Frame Book

1. Fold a sheet of paper (8 1/2" x 11") in half like a *hamburger*.

2. Open the *hamburger* and gently roll one side of the *hamburger* toward the *valley*. Try not to crease the roll.

3. Cut a rectangle out of the middle of the rolled side of the paper leaving a half-inch border, forming a frame.

4. Fold another sheet of paper (8 1/2" x 11") in half like a *hamburger*. Apply glue to the inside border of the picture frame and place the folded, uncut sheet of paper inside.

Use this book to feature a person, place, or thing. Inside the picture frames, glue photographs, magazine pictures, computer-generated graphs, or have students sketch pictures. This book has three inside pages for writing and recording notes.

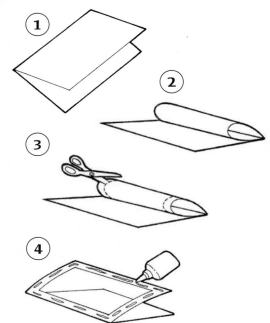

Display Case

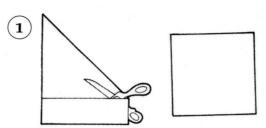

1. Make a *taco* fold and cut off the rectangular tab formed. This will result in a square.

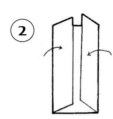

2. Fold the square into a *shutter fold*.

3. Unfold and fold the square into another *shutter fold* perpendicular to the direction of the first. This will form a small square at each of the four corners of the sheet of paper.

4. As illustrated, cut along two fold lines on opposite sides of the large square.

5. Collapse in and glue the cut tabs to form an open box.

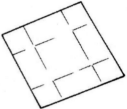

How to Make a Lid

Fold another open-sided box using a square of paper one-half inch larger than the square used to make the first box. This will make a lid that fits snugly over the display box. *Example:* If the base is made out of an 8 1/2" paper square, then make the top out of a 9" square.

Cut a hole out of the lid and cover the opening with a cut piece of acetate used on overhead projectors. Heavy, clear plastic wrap or scraps from a laminating machine also will work. Secure the clear plastic sheet to the inside of the lid with glue or tape.

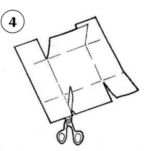
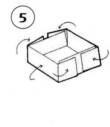

NOTE: *You can place polystyrene foam or quilt batting in the boxes to display insects. Glue the boxes onto a sheet of cardboard to make them strong enough to display rocks and minerals.*

U.S. AIR FORCE
BRONZE STAR MEDAL

LIBERTY STANDING
HALF DOLLAR (Silver)
SCARCE
1939-S $3.50

RARE U.S. CURRENCY

Billboard Project

1. Fold all pieces of the same size of paper in half like *hamburgers*.

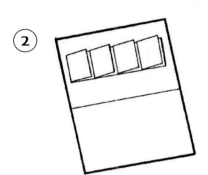

2. Place a line of glue at the top and bottom of one side of each folded billboard section and glue them edge-to-edge on a background paper or project board. If glued correctly, all doors will open from right to left.

3. Pictures, dates, and text go on the front of each billboard section. When opened, writing or drawings can be seen on the inside left of each section. The base, or the part glued to the background, is perfect for in-depth information or definitions.

Use for time lines or sequencing data, such as events in a war, presidents of the United States, or ratification of states.

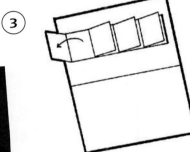

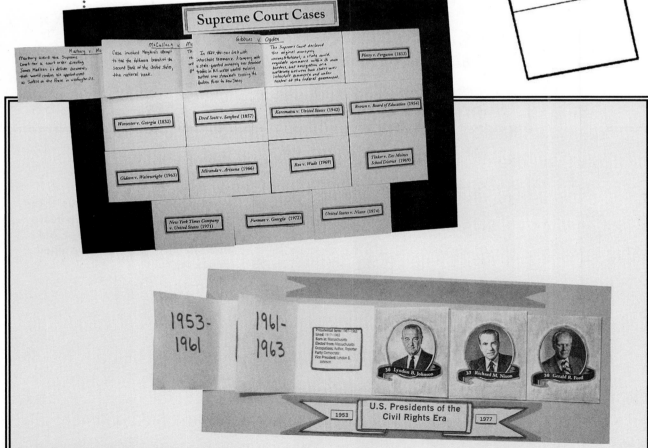

Project Board with Tabs

1. Draw a large illustration or a series of small illustrations or write on the front of one of the pieces of selected-size paper.

2. Pinch and slightly fold the paper at the point where a tab is desired on the illustrated project board. Cut into the paper on the fold. Cut straight in, then cut up to form an "L." When the paper is unfolded, it will form a tab with an illustration on the front.

3. After all tabs have been cut, glue this front sheet onto a second piece of paper. Place glue around all four edges and in the middle, away from tabs.

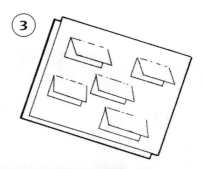

Write or draw under the tabs. If the project is made as a bulletin board using butcher paper, quarter and half-sheets of paper can be glued under the tabs.

Sentence Strips

1. *Take two sheets of paper (8 1/2" x 11") and fold into hamburgers. Cut along the fold lines making four half sheets. (Use as many half sheets as necessary for additional pages to your book.)*

2. Fold each sheet in half like a *hot dog.*

3. Place the folds side-by-side and staple them together on the left side.

4. 1" from the stapled edge, cut the front page of each folded section up to the *mountain* top. These cuts form flaps that can be raised and lowered.

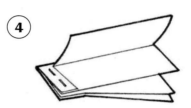

To make a half-cover, use a sheet of construction paper one inch longer than the book. Glue the back of the last sheet to the construction paper strip leaving one inch, on the left side, to fold over and cover the original staples. Staple this half-cover in place.

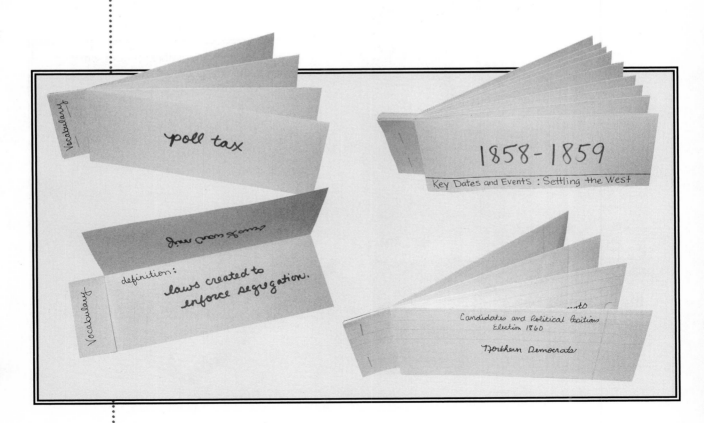

Sentence-Strip Holder

1. Fold a sheet of paper (8 1/2" x 11") in half like a *hamburger*.

2. Open the *hamburger* and fold the two outer edges toward the *valley*. This forms a *shutter fold*.

3. Fold one of the inside edges of the *shutter* back to the outside fold. This fold forms a floppy "L."

4. Glue the floppy L-tab down to the base so that it forms a strong, straight L-tab.

5. Glue the other *shutter* side to the front of this L-tab. This forms a tent that is the backboard for the flashcards or student work to be displayed.

6. Fold the edge of the L-tab up one quarter to one half to form a lip that will keep the student work from slipping off the holder.

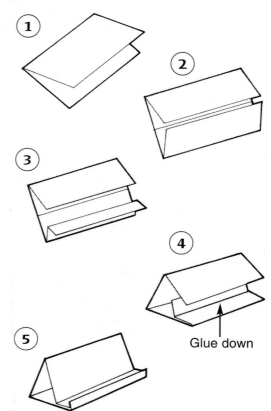

Glue down

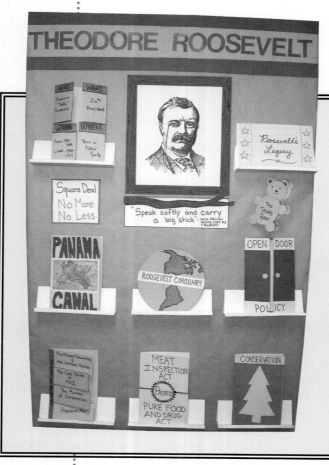

Use these holders to display student work on a table, or glue them onto a bulletin board to make it interactive.

Three-Pocket Book

1. Fold a horizontal sheet of paper (11" x 17") into thirds.

2. Fold the bottom edge up two inches and crease well. Glue the outer edges of the two inch tab to create three pockets.

3. Label each pocket. Use to hold notes taken on index cards or quarter sheets of paper.

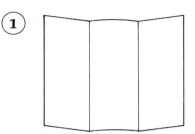

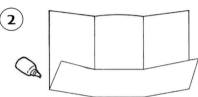

Forward-Backward Book

1. Stack three or more sheets of paper. On the top sheet trace a large circle.

2. With the papers still stacked, cut out the circles.

3. Staple the paper circles together along the left-hand side to create a book.

4. Label the cover and takes notes on the pages that open to the right.

5. Turn the book upside down and label the back. Takes notes on the pages that open to the right.

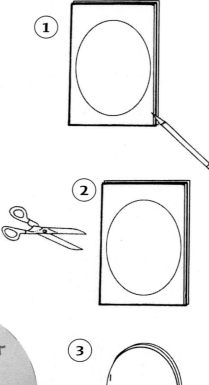

Front

Compare and Contrast

General Nathaniel Greene

Back

Compare and Contrast

Benedict Arnold

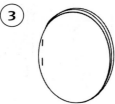

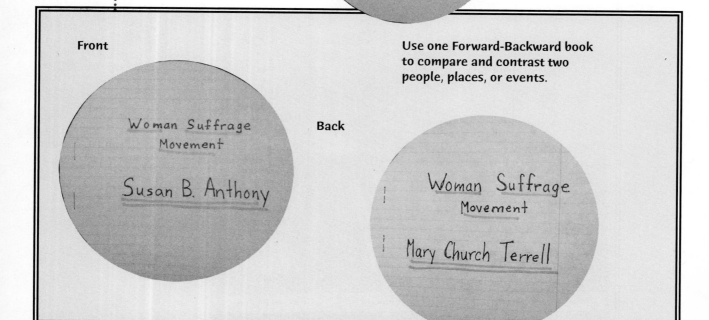

Front

Woman Suffrage Movement

Susan B. Anthony

Back

Woman Suffrage Movement

Mary Church Terrell

Use one Forward-Backward book to compare and contrast two people, places, or events.

Activities for

High School
American History

T he pages that follow contain Foldable activities to use for key topics in high school American history—from important issues in the founding days of the American Republic right through to the present. For teachers' convenience, the topics are correlated to chapters in *The American Republic Since 1877, The American Vision,* and *American Odyssey.* (See page 44.)

For each topic, there is a summary and three Foldable activities, with instructions and illustrations for students. Students review subject material as they create the Foldables. Students can then use their Foldables to prepare for classroom and standardized tests.

Correlation to Glencoe American History

FOLDABLES TOPIC	AMERICAN VISION	AMERICAN REPUBLIC	AMERICAN ODYSSEY
1. Geography and History	NGS*	NGS*	1
2. Converging Cultures	1–4	1	2
3. Spanish, French, and English Settlements in America	2	1	2
4. Regions and Colonies: New England, Mid-Atlantic, South	2–3	2	2
5. The American Revolution	4	3	3
6. The Articles of Confederation and the Constitution	5	3	4
7. The Emergence of Political Parties	6	4	4
8. A National Economy	7	5	5
9. Social Reform	8	5	5
10. Manifest Destiny	9	5	5
11. Causes of the Civil War	10	6	6
12. The Civil War: Strategies and Outcomes	11	7	6
13. Reconstruction	12	7	6
14. African Americans, 1890-1920	15–16	11	9
15. Settling the West	13	8	7
16. Industrialization	14	9	7
17. Immigration and Urbanization	15	10	8
18. Labor Movement	14	9	7
19. Populism	16	11	7
20. Imperialism	17	12	7
21. The Progressives	18	13	8
22. The Progressive Spirit and the Presidency	17–18	13	9
23. World War I	19	14	10
24. Women's Suffrage	18	13	8
25. The Jazz Age	20	15	12
26. The Postwar Economic Boom	21	16	11
27. The Great Depression	22	17	13
28. The New Deal	23	18	14
29. World War II	24	19	15
30. World War II: The Home Front	25	20	16
31. The Cold War	26	21	17
32. McCarthyism	26	21	19
33. The Affluent Society	27	22	18
34. Johnson and the Great Society	28	23	21
35. The Civil Rights Movement	29	24	20
36. The Vietnam War	30	25	23
37. Voices of Protest	31	26	22
38. Nixon and Watergate	32	27	24
39. Reagan and the New Conservatism	33	28	25
40. The New Century	34	29	26

* National Geographic Society Geography

Geography and History

TOPIC SUMMARY

Geographical characteristics are basic to how history has developed over time. They influence where people settle and their migration patterns. They also influence the kind of economy that develops and thus to an extent, the kind of social classes that come about. Geographers have established five broad themes to cover their discipline: location; place; movement; human/environment; and region. Each of these can be related to historical events or developments.

Summarizing Geographical Themes

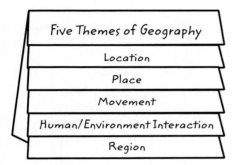

🎧 Layered Book

Students should create a Layered-Look Book to record and explain the five themes of geography. Students will write the title on the top-most tab and label the five smaller tabs with the five themes. Each will be explained under the appropriate tab, with at least one specific example for a certain time period. Students can use their notes to explain the history of their own region.

Materials Needed: three sheets of 8.5" x 11" paper, stapler or glue.

Drawing Conclusions

Themes	Geography of the U.S.	Influences on History
Location		
Place		
Movement		
Human/ Environment Interaction		
Region		

🎧 Folded Table

Students can sharpen their ability to draw conclusions by using this Foldable to show geography's influence on history. Students should label rows with the five geographical themes. In the columns, students can identify a *specific* geographical location, place, movement, human/environmental interaction or region. In the second column, they must review the text or conduct research to identify the influence. Urge students to spread their examples across different time periods.

Materials Needed: one sheet of 8.5" x 11" paper.

Determine What History and Geography Have in Common

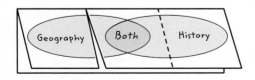

◖ Three-Tab Book

Have students use this design to promote their understanding of how geography and history are related. Students should review text material on the links between geographical and historical elements. Overlap can be detected in all five geography themes, but Human/Environment interaction is a theme where the overlap is easily seen.

Materials Needed: one sheet of 8.5" x 11" paper, scissors.

Converging Cultures: Native American, African, and European

TOPIC SUMMARY

North America would become a continent of many peoples, many ethnicities. Native Americans arrived much earlier than Europeans or Africans, occupying parts of North America by 10,000 B.C. Each major group brought with them customs they adapted to the new land—Native Americans, for example, were nomadic when they arrived in North America and their cultures often developed accordingly. When the three groups made contact, cultural changes and cultural conflict was the result.

Describing North American Cultural Groups

North American Settlement	Dates of Arrival in North America	Region(s) of Settlement	Major Cultural Traits
Native Americans			
Africans			
Europeans			

🎧 Folded Table

Have students review text material on Native Americans, Europeans, and Africans from the earliest times through the colonial period. They should take notes on each of the three groups for the early period of their history in America. Then have them create a Foldable Table to record the data.

Materials Needed: one 8.5" by 11" sheet of paper.

Identifying Cultural Interaction

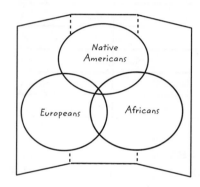

🎧 Trifold with Venn Diagram

After having completed the Foldable on converging cultures, students should find specific examples of interaction among the three major North American groups. Students will find it useful to scan all chapters for the period from 1600 to 1776 to find examples for this Trifold Foldable.

Materials Needed: one 8.5" by 11" sheet of paper.

Sequencing Events of Different Groups

Timeline	1500	1600	1700	1800
Native Americans				
Europeans				
Africans				

◖ Folded Table

In studying early North American history, students can record key dates for each group in chronological order. Parallel time line allows students to quickly see how the history of each group compares or interacts with the history of another. Students should enter the major events for each group on three parallel time lines. Time lines should start in 1500 and end at about 1800.

Materials Needed: one 8.5" by 11" sheet of paper.

Spanish, French, and English Settlements in America

TOPIC SUMMARY

The European settlement that is usually identified as beginning with Columbus' voyage had a profound effect on American political institutions and social classes. In reading about the colonial period, students will learn about the differing goals and experiences of Spanish, French, and English settlers. The fortunes of each nation's settlements in the New World were also different. In the end, it was English colonists and English settlements that played the dominant role in shaping the new nation.

Describing National Groups

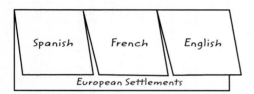

👤 Three-Tab Book

By organizing information about Europeans in the New World in a Three-Tab Foldable, students can better understand their comparative experiences. They can also better understand the reasons for the relative success or failure of each settler group. Have students prepare a Three-Tab Foldable with each group listed on the top tab. Inside students should list information on each group: their purpose in colonizing; major colonies; and homeland values or traditions they brought to the New World.

Materials Needed: one sheet of 8.5" by 11" paper, scissors.

Analyzing Colonization

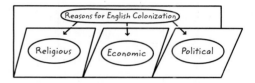

👤 Concept-Map Book

From the earliest times, European colonists had myriad reasons for sailing off to a strange new land. The reasons English colonists settled on the eastern coast of America can be grouped under three categories—religious, economic, and political. Have students complete this type of Foldable to highlight the different motivations. For each, students should list specific examples, including individual colonies, or the actions of a specific leader or group.

Materials Needed: **one** sheet of 8.5" by 11" paper, scissors.

Identifying Colonial Experiments

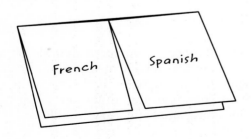

👈 Two-Tab Book

Students need to be able to analyze the colonial successes and failures in the French and Spanish experience. Students should carefully read text matter on each group, noting examples of successes and failures as they go. In completing their Two-Tab Foldable, they may want to consider their ability to attract settlers or adapt to the environment, among other things.

Materials Needed: sheet of 8.5" by 11" paper, scissors.

Regions and Colonies:
New England, Mid-Atlantic, South

TOPIC SUMMARY

The colonies established along the eastern seaboard varied by region and type. Colonies were founded as joint-stock colonies, royal colonies, or proprietary colonies. The motives for founding a colony often helped determine the kind of government that developed. Economic activities influenced the kind of social classes that developed—whether power was concentrated in one class, and how social classes interacted.

Categorizing Colonies

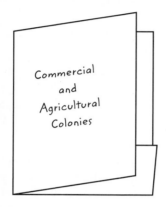

🖐 Pocket Book

Have students create a Pocket Book Foldable to make distinctions between commercial and agricultural colonies. In the pocket for each type, students should prepare 3" x 5" index cards naming colonies which fit. Index cards should report on: the founding period, its type of government, and the types of products produced.

Materials Needed: one sheet of 8.5" by 11" paper, glue.

Compare and Contrast

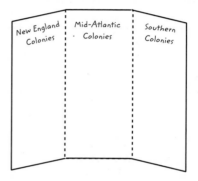

🖐 Trifold Book

Have students prepare a Trifold Foldable on the three distinctive colonial regions. When the Trifold is closed, *American Colonies, 1760s,* will appear on the front. The three folds inside will display comparative information: approximate population, its ethnic make-up, geography, government institutions, social class structure, and type of economy.

Materials Needed: one sheet of 8.5" by 11" paper.

Analyzing Puritan Life

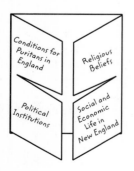

🖐 Four-Door Book

Have students prepare a foldable that will prepare them for analytical questions on the Puritans in America. Students can review their text material and research Puritans on the Internet, taking notes for their foldable. The four "doors" will be labeled: conditions for Puritans in England; religious beliefs; political institutions; social and economic life in New England. Bulleted lists inside will address these sub-topics.

Materials Needed: one sheet of 8.5" by 11" paper, scissors.

The American Revolution:
The Causes and Course of the War

TOPIC SUMMARY

The American Revolution, one of the most important and intriguing topics in American history, was born out of a complex chain of events. During the Revolution, new political thinking and new political institutions came about and both have continued to influence world events. Students can also follow the course of the war to understand why the mighty British Empire was unable to defeat the feisty colonists who demanded independence.

Comparing British Legislation

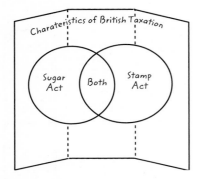

☊ Trifold Book

Two laws that roused the colonists' fury at the British were the Sugar Act and the Stamp Act. Have students construct a Trifold Foldable to make a close comparison between the two pieces of legislation. A Venn diagram of overlapping circles can be drawn to show characteristics that differ and those that are the same.

Materials Needed: one sheet of 8.5" by 11" paper.

Cause and Effect

Road to War	CAUSES	EFFECTS
Proclamation of 1763		
Stamp Act		
Townshend Acts		
Boston Tea Party		
Coercive Acts		

☊ Folded Table

Students should be able to clearly identify the causes and effects of key events of the Revolutionary period. Have students create a Folded Table Foldable for events leading to the war. Causes and effects should be identified in two columns for each of the following: Proclamation of 1763, the Stamp Act, the Townshend Acts, Boston Tea Party, the Coercive Acts.

Materials Needed: one sheet of 8.5" by 11" paper.

Generalizing on the American Revolution

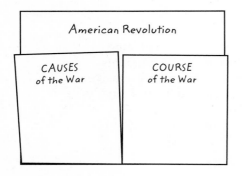

☋ Concept-Map Book

The causes of the Revolution and the course of the Revolutionary War involved multiple factors and events. By creating this Foldable students see the big picture. Have students select the *most important causes* of the war and list them in a flow chart format inside one-half of the Concept-Map Foldable. The other half of the Foldable can be used in the same fashion to reflect battle outcomes during the war's course.

Materials Needed: one sheet of 8.5" by 11" paper, scissors.

The Articles of Confederation and the Constitution

TOPIC SUMMARY

The essential qualities of American government came about through trial and error in the period from 1781 to 1789 when the country was governed under the Articles of Confederation. That period made clearer to Americans what kind of government they wanted. The biggest distinction between the Articles of Confederation and the Constitution was whether the central or state governments should have sovereign power over various functions.

Evaluating the Articles of Confederation

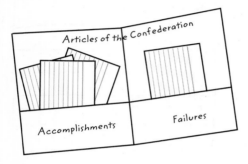

🎧 Pocket Book

Have students review their text or other sources to identify the key features of the Articles of the Confederation. As students take notes, they should record the accomplishments and failures of the Articles. They can then prepare this Foldable in order to reflect their assessment of the Articles of Confederation.

Materials Needed: one sheet of 8.5" by 11" paper.

Summarizing the Constitutional Debates

Ratification	Views	Campaign	Outcome
Federalists			
Anti-Federalists			

🎧 Folded Table

Key issues during the ratification debate were argued by the Federalists and Anti-Federalists. Have students create this Foldable to summarize three aspects of the Federalist and Anti-Federalist debate: their views, their campaigns, and the result in the Constitution of their specific positions.

Materials Needed: one sheet of 8.5" by 11" paper.

Analyzing Constitutional Powers

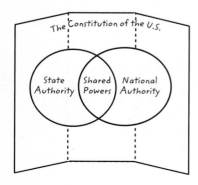

☝ Trifold Book

Have students analyze the Constitution by listing where various functions of government lie. Students should first take notes to understand powers exclusive to the state, powers exclusive to the nation, and, finally, shared powers. This information can be displayed conveniently in a Trifold Foldable with a Venn diagram.

Materials Needed: one sheet of 8.5" by 11" paper.

The Emergence of Political Parties

TOPIC SUMMARY

Political "faction" caused suspicion among the Founding Fathers. They worried that organized parties would cause disunity and instability. Yet without parties to represent groups with different interests and opinions, no republic would succeed in representing everyone. After 1789, two parties formed, the Federalists and the Democratic-Republicans. Their views on central versus state government were similar to the views of Federalists and Anti-Federalists.

Comparing Parties

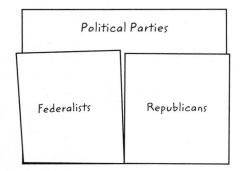

🎧 Concept Map Book

After students have reviewed the text on Federalists and Republicans in the early period, have them prepare a Concept-Map Foldable. Students may choose different points of comparison, but they should compare the points, party to party. Some examples might be: attitude toward national expansion; the social or occupational groups which favored each party; banking policy; taxation policy.

Materials Needed: one sheet of 8.5" by 11" paper, scissors.

Describing: Journal Writing

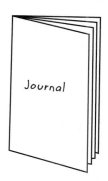

🎧 Bound Book

Remind students that during the early republic leaders like Washington or John Adams faced unprecedented difficulties, that Cabinet and Congress were untried, and that citizen expectations and duties were not always clear. Ask students to pick a certain crisis in the presidency of Washington or Adams. They should then write a four-page journal entry for either man.

Materials Needed: one sheet of 8.5" by 11" paper, scissors.

Analyzing

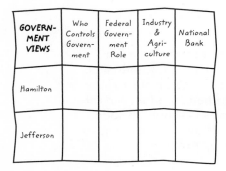

🌀 Folded Table

The views of Hamilton and Jefferson are often counterpoised because of their influence on the country's early political life. Hamilton dominated the ideas of the Federalists, while Jefferson molded the ideas of the Republicans. Have students create a Folded Table that compares their views on different subjects, for example: who should control government; the role of industry; the role of agriculture; national bank; the role of federal government.

Materials Needed: one sheet of 8.5" by 11" paper.

A National Economy

TOPIC SUMMARY

The growth of a national economy strengthened the sense of nationalism among Americans. Through commerce, citizens had more common interests and greater contact. New roads, canals, and eventually the railroads linked markets across regions. Even so, the stronger growth of industry in the North, and the expansion of slavery in the South contributed to regional identities with different values. Those differences led to the Civil War.

Comparing and Contrasting

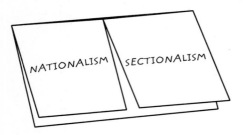

🎧 Two-Tab Book

Have students prepare a Two-Tab Foldable to compare and contrast nationalism and sectionalism. Students should review their text and prepare a list to record in their Foldable. It should include: a brief characterization of each "ism"; and, significant events occurring between 1820 and 1860 that reflected nationalism versus sectionalism.

Materials Needed: one sheet of 8.5" by 11" paper, scissors.

Analyzing Economies

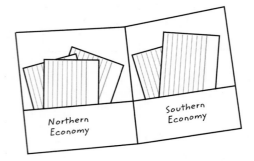

🎧 Pocket Book

Even in colonial times, the economies of the North and the South differed. These differences became more pronounced with slavery's growth. Have students create a Pocket Book Foldable on the two economies. Students should review their text and conduct their own research on measures of economic growth, such as, population growth from 1800 to 1850, number of railroad miles, and amount of manufactured imports. The information should be placed on index cards and placed in the pockets.

Materials Needed: one sheet of 8.5" by 11" paper, glue.

Summarizing Transportation Systems

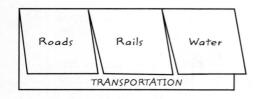

🅒 Three-Tab Book

Advances and innovations in transportation were concentrated in three areas: roads, railroads, and travel by water. Have students create a Three-Tab Foldable that lists important facts for each category. In a bulleted list, students should include the dates of any relevant inventions, legislation, or building projects. They should also describe the location and routes of major transportation networks.

Materials Needed: one sheet of 8.5" by 11" paper, scissors.

Social Reform

TOPIC SUMMARY

Social reformers in early 19th century America set up some of the enduring educational and philanthropic institutions in the country. Among them were public schools, more humane prisons and mental institutions, and new religious communities. Most reform efforts were inspired by the religious enthusiasm of the Great Awakening. Ever since that time, private philanthropy has been an American tradition, with idealistic people working to improving conditions for other Americans.

Summarizing Lives

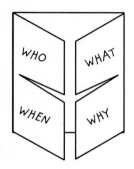

⋔ Four-Door Book

Have students prepare a Four-Door Foldable as a way of summarizing basic data on a reformer of their choice, such as Horace Mann, Lyman Beecher, or Harriet Beecher Stowe. Students may expand on their information by conducting an Internet search. Under each of the "doors," students should record information that thoroughly answers the questions, Who, What, When and Why.

Materials Needed: one sheet of 8.5" by 11" paper, scissors.

Identifying Reform Movements

⋔ Four-Tab Book

Have students create a Four-Tab Book in order to identify the major reform streams in American society in the early 19th century. For each reform movement, students should report on: when it began, its causes, its leadership, its accomplishments.

Materials Needed: one sheet of 8.5" by 11" paper, scissors.

Interpretating Social Realities

⊂ Bound Book

Students should gather information about the life of an enslaved person who served in the masters' house, rather than working in the fields. For library or Web searches, search terms might include *house servants* or *domestic servants*. Students should write a journal for one day in the life of such a person, recording it in a Bound Book Foldable. Students will want to notice the kind of relations house servants had with their owners, and with other enslaved people.

Materials Needed: one sheet of 8.5" by 11" paper, scissors.

Manifest Destiny

TOPIC SUMMARY

The nation expanded westward with the Louisiana Purchase and the acquisition of Texas and other territories west of the Appalachian Mountains. This expansion set off a period of rapid economic growth. Railroads, canals, and roads were a major support to commerce and trade between the East and West. As white Americans prospered and moved west, however, Native Americans faced displacement and exploitation.

Cause and Effect

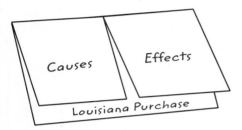

Two-Tab Book

Ask students to work with a partner to create a Two-Tab Foldable showing cause-and-effect relationships. Have students select events that led to territorial expansion, such as with the Louisiana Purchase, the Treaty of Guadalupe Hidalgo or the Gadsden Purchase. Ask students to identify two or more causes of each event, and two effects of the event.

Materials Needed: one sheet of 8.5" by 11" paper.

What, When, Where, Why?

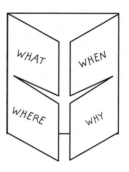

Four-Door Book

Have students research the development of early transportation routes. Encourage them to include different methods of transport that were useful in different sections of the country, such as the Wilderness Road, Erie Canal, Oregon Trail, and the Baltimore and Ohio Railroad. Ask students to record key facts about each route in a Four-Door Foldable under: What, When, Where, and Why.

Materials Needed: one sheet of 8.5" x 11" paper.

Analyzing Changes Over Time

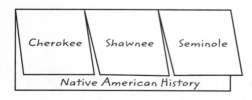

Three-Tab Book

Have students choose three Native American groups whose land was taken due to the pressure of white settlement. Inside each tab, students should use the top portion to write each group's name, location, population, and how they used the land. On the bottom portion of the inside, they should write: each group's new location after being driven off the land; where the white settlers were from; and, how settlers used the land.

Materials Needed: one sheet of 8.5" by 11" paper.

Causes of the Civil War

TOPIC SUMMARY

As slavery grew, so did opposition to it. The North and South had become more distinct over time in every way—socially, economically, and politically. These differences made compromise over slavery even more difficult and tensions grew. Finally, it was territorial expansion which brought war. The status of slavery in each new territory was intensely debated. The North did not want a slave-state majority in Congress any more than the South wanted a free-state majority.

Analyzing Watershed Events

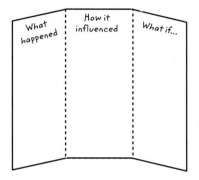

○ Trifold Book

Ask students to choose one of the following to research: the Fugitive Slave Act, the Dred Scott Decision, the Lincoln-Douglas Debates, the Missouri Compromise, the Kansas-Nebraska Act, or John Brown's Raid. Have each student write a three-part account of the event in a Trifold Book: what happened; how it influenced events leading to the Civil War; what might have happened if the event had turned out differently.

Materials Needed: one sheet of 8.5" x 11" paper.

Distinguishing Different Opinions

Arguments	Basis of Position	Persons & Events	Outcome/ Reaction
Pro-Slavery			
Anti-Slavery			

○ Folded Chart

Have students make a chart showing the reasons behind pro-slavery and anti-slavery opinions before the Civil War. In one column, students should describe the basis of each position—whether it is an economic, moral, constitutional, or legal argument. In another column, they should describe a person or event that reflects that position (for example, John Brown's raid, the Dred Scott decision, or the nullification crisis). In the third column, students should note the outcome or reaction to the person or event.

Materials Needed: one sheet of 8.5" x 11" paper.

Organizing Geographical Information

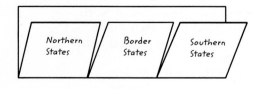

☚ Three-Tab Book

Have students make a Venn diagram on a Three-Tab Foldable and list the states in the following categories: Northern, Border, and Confederate Southern. Inside each tab, students should list facts about the legal status and living conditions of African Americans. Encourage students to consider such things as families, educational and economic opportunities, and citizens' rights.

Materials Needed: one sheet of 8.5" x 11" paper.

The Civil War: Strategies and Outcomes

TOPIC SUMMARY

The Union and the Confederacy were vastly different in population, resources, and industrial capacity. While the South was largely a rural agricultural society with a few major cities, the North was rapidly industrializing. A growing railroad network linked its numerous urban centers; a larger population and greater financial resources gave the North the advantage in a prolonged war. However, the South had a superior group of military leaders and the tactical advantage of defending its own soil.

Charting Campaigns

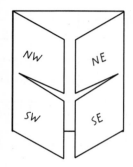

Four-Door Book

Have students research major Civil War battles that took place in each region of the United States. Ask students to list the battles, such as Gettysburg (NE), Atlanta (SE), Vicksburg (SW), and Shiloh (NW) on the outside of a Four-Door Foldable. Have students describe each battle on the inside of the door, and then summarize its importance in the area behind the door.

Materials Needed: one 8.5" x 11" sheet of paper.

Outlining Compromise Efforts

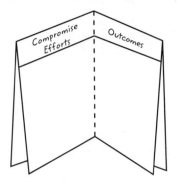

Half Book

Students can better grasp the depth of regional differences by understanding the failure of compromise efforts before the Civil War. Ask students to complete a chart showing the series of compromise attempts that were made. Students should describe each compromise effort in the left-hand column. In the right-hand column, they should describe the outcomes.

Materials Needed: one 8.5" x 11" sheet of paper.

Comparing Economies

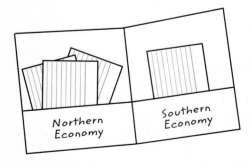

Pocket Book

Have students create this Foldable in order to examine characteristics of the economies of North and South. Students can select their own characteristics but they should be sure to report on both regions for any given characteristic. Characteristics might include: total population, coal and iron resources, the number of major cities, and railroad miles.

Materials Needed: one 8.5" x 11" sheet of paper, glue.

Reconstruction

TOPIC SUMMARY

Deep divisions remained after the Civil War about how to restore the states of the former Confederacy to the Union. Lincoln's assassination interfered and his relatively lenient approach was not adopted. Instead, Radical Republicans in Congress succeeded in forcing harsher requirements on the defeated states. Once Democrats regained control of state governments in the South, however, black codes and Jim Crow laws reversed many of the gains of African American emancipation.

Summarizing Legislation

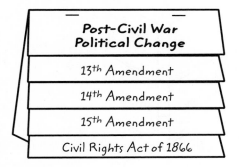

🖑 Layered-Look Book

Have students list on this Foldable the major provisions of the following four pieces of legislation: the Thirteenth, Fourteenth, and Fifteenth Amendments to the Constitution and the Civil Rights Act of 1866. Students can use this Foldable to make a presentation to the class on the effect these changes in the law had on the everyday lives of Americans.

Materials Needed: two sheets of 8.5" x 11" paper.

Contrasting Before and After

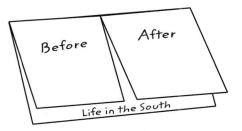

🖑 Two-Tab Book

Ask students to collect information about life in the South before and after the Civil War, listing the most important facts in a Two-Tab Foldable. Encourage students to include information about all levels of Southern society—rich and poor, white and black, native-born and immigrant—and note how conditions changed for each group.

Materials Needed: two sheets of 8.5" x 11" paper.

Comparing Plans

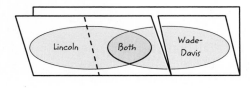

👉 Three-Tab Book

Ask students to outline the main features of Lincoln's plan for Reconstruction on one side of a Venn diagram and the main features of the Wade-Davis Plan on the opposite side. Have students compare the two plans and write their common features in the center section. Encourage students to consider the role of Lincoln's successor, Andrew Johnson, in dealing with Congress. Have students write a paragraph describing how these conflicts were resolved.

Materials Needed: one sheet of 8.5" x 11" paper.

African Americans, 1890-1920

TOPIC SUMMARY

A new generation of African American leaders emerged after the Reconstruction era. Educational opportunities expanded, and a few African Americans rose to prominence in science and certain professions. While emancipation improved the lives of some former slaves, legal restrictions and entrenched attitudes kept most African Americans poor and outside the political process.

Defining Key Terms

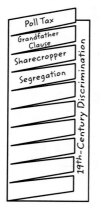

🎧 Vocabulary Book

Have students list the following terms on the outside tabs of a 10-tab booklet: *poll tax, grandfather clause, sharecropper, segregation, Jim Crow, lynching,* and *Exodusters.* Students should look up each term and write the definition under the tab for the term. Ask students to identify three more terms related to 19th-century discrimination against African Americans to complete the booklet.

Materials Needed: one sheet of 8.5" x 11" paper.

Researching Biographical Information

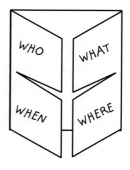

🎧 Four-Door Book

Ask students to research the lives of African Americans who shaped events between 1890 and 1920. Examples might include Booker T. Washington, Ida B. Wells, and W.E.B. Du Bois, but encourage students to investigate other figures. Then have students list facts about each person in a Four-Door Foldable under the headings Who, What, When, and Where.

Materials Needed: one sheet of 8.5" x 11" paper.

Contrasting Discrimination in North and South

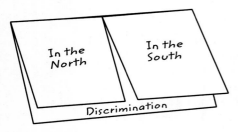

◖ Two-Tab Book

Have students create a Two-Tab book, labeling one "In the North" and the other "In the South." Ask students to find and list examples of different forms of discrimination against African Americans and where they occurred.

Materials Needed: one sheet of 8.5" x 11" paper.

Settling the West: Displacing Native Americans

TOPIC SUMMARY

As white settlers pushed west, they forced Native Americans even farther west, depriving them of their hunting grounds. The whites' destruction of buffalo herds was fatal to the life of Plains Indians. Many conflicts between settlers and Native American groups took place, and in 1867, Congress established the first reservations. Native Americans often resisted. Later, the government tried an assimilation policy, offering Native Americans homestead allotments. This too proved a failure.

Summarizing Displacement

🔖 Sentence Strips

Students can create a Sentence Strip Foldable to represent how white settlers displaced the Native American population. For the events they choose, students can create as many flip books as needed. The name and date of an event, such as the Homestead Act, Sand Creek Massacre, or Battle of Wounded Knee, should be written on the front of each strip, with a brief explanation of how the event led to displacement underneath.

Materials Needed: two or more sheets of 8.5" by 11" paper, stapler, scissors.

Sequencing Native American History

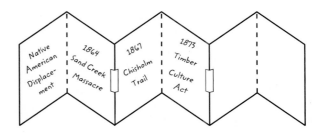

🔖 Accordion Book

Students can create a usable time line by using the Accordion Book Foldable. Have students list important events in Native American-white settler conflicts, using as many sheets of paper as they need to complete the time line. The time line will be annotated, that is, there will be brief notes on the event under the date.

Materials Needed: three or more sheets of 8.5" by 11" paper, scissors, glue.

Railroads: Cause and Effect

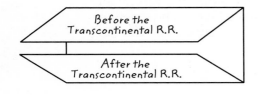

🔖 Shutter Fold

The transcontinental railroad affected many aspects of American life—the economy, settlement in the West, the life of Native Americans, and farming. Have students review related material and create a shutter fold to display the aspects they choose.

Students should describe the situation *before* the transcontinental railroad was built, and *after* its completion.

Materials Needed: one sheet of 8.5" by 11" of paper.

Industrialization

TOPIC SUMMARY

Industrialization may well be the most important historical transition for any society. When a society changes from a rural to an industrial economy, almost every aspect of the society is affected—for example, a country's economic wealth, its urbanization, the make-up of different social classes, the role of family members, and educational opportunities. In the United States the greatest impact of the Industrial Revolution came after the Civil War.

Categorizing Factors in the American Industrial Revolution.

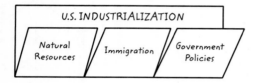

🎧 Concept-Map Book

Have students address the factors that promoted industrialization in the United States by creating a Concept-Map Foldable. The students should review their text on the topic and list as many factors as they can, such as this nation's rich natural resources, or large immigrant workforce. Inside their concept book, they should elaborate on each factor. A second Concept-Map Foldable could be made to accommodate more than three factors promoting industrialization.

Materials Needed: one sheet of 8.5" by 11" paper.

Industrialization and the Civil War

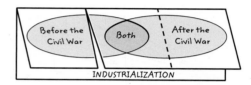

🎧 Three-Tab Book

Students should review their text on how the Civil War transformed the nature of industry in the United States. They can promote their analytical thinking by creating a Three-Tab foldable with a Venn diagram. Elements of industry before the Civil War can be listed under one tab, elements of industry after the Civil War under another, and shared industrial or economic elements under the middle tab.

Materials Needed: one sheet of 8.5" by 11" paper.

Compare and Contrast

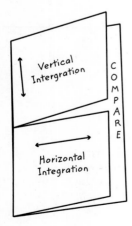

⭲ Two-Tab Book

In the highly competitive environment of late 19th-century business, big businesses merged to dominate the market for their products. Have students create a Two-Tab Foldable to highlight the two major ways mergers were accomplished: horizontal and vertical integration. Underneath each tabs, students should write a brief definition of each merger type, along with a small organizational chart to represent its organization.

Materials Needed: one sheet of 8.5" by 11" paper.

Immigration and Urbanization

TOPIC SUMMARY

From the end of the Civil War through the 1890s, the nation throbbed with change and prosperity. The American population grew, as did factories and cities, while settlements expanded rapidly in the West. Inventors and scientists contributed to new industrial processes, increased productivity, and improved communication. There were many underlying causes for these dramatic developments. Two of the most important were immigration and urbanization.

Analyzing Immigration and Urbanization

RESEARCH	CAUSES	EFFECTS
Immigration		
Urbanization		

🎧 Folded Table

Students can clarify their understanding of how immigration and urbanization are related by making this Foldable. They should create a four-celled Folded Table that lists the causes and effects of immigration and urbanization. In each cell, they should list as many causes and effects of each phenomenon as possible, adding approximate dates where appropriate.

Materials Needed: one sheet of 8.5" by 11" paper, scissors

Comparing an Agricultural and an Industrial Economy

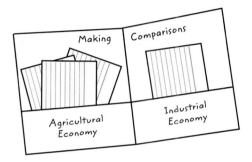

🎧 Pocket Book

Contemporary urban America is very different from the days when the nation was made up of farmers and people living in small towns. For example, some ways in which a rural and urban society differ is reflected in the types of occupations, level of income, and different social classes and social relations among them. Have students create a pocket foldable and then be as specific as possible in describing all the possible differences. These will be listed on index cards for placement in the pockets.

Materials Needed: one sheet of 8.5" by 11" paper, index cards, glue

Categorizing Urban Social Classes

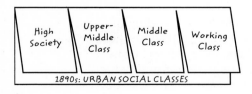

⬅ Four-Tab Book

Students can create a Four-Tab Foldable to help them review urban social classes. They should focus on either late 19th-century or contemporary American society. For each social class, they should be as specific as possible in listing characteristics of each group, for example: occupations, approximate wealth, and political and social attitudes.

Materials Needed: two sheets of 8.5" by 11" paper, stapler or glue.

The Labor Movement

TOPIC SUMMARY

As industrialization took hold, workers faced not only new and dangerous working conditions, but often powerful employers. Since employers had a huge labor pool available to them, they had a powerful bargaining position, while labor was weak. Gradually unions formed and with power in numbers they could bring pressure on employers to achieve better wages, shorter hours, and safer working conditions.

Defining the Labor Movement

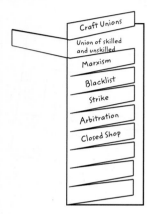

🔵 Vocabulary Book

Students can create their own review sheet on this topic by making a Vocabulary Book Foldable, with leading terms and/or proper names associated with the labor movement. Students can cull terms from a brief re-reading of their text. Examples of terms and proper names include: *craft unions, industrial unions, Marxism, blacklist, strike, arbitration, closed shop, Knights of Labor, Samuel Gompers.*

Materials Needed: one sheet of 8.5" by 11" paper, scissors.

Categorizing Labor Events, 1869-1895

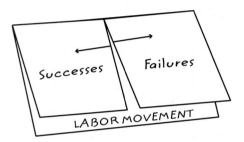

🔵 Two-Tab Book

In reviewing material on the labor movement of the late 19th century, students should take notes on setbacks and advances workers experienced. Students can retain this information by placing notable events or developments under two headings—*Successes* and *Failures*—in a Two-Tab Foldable.

Materials Needed: one sheet of 8.5" by 11" paper, scissors.

Comparing Labor and Farm Goals

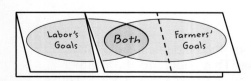

🔵 Three-Tab Book

Students can increase their understanding of labor unions by comparing their goals with those of farmers. Factory workers and farmers began organizing to achieve group goals at roughly the same time. Have students create a Three-Tab Book with a Venn diagram to list the goals of the labor movement and of farmers' organizations.

Materials Needed: one sheet of 8.5" by 11" paper, scissors.

Populism

TOPIC SUMMARY

From the 1870s to the 1890s, the farmers' movement known as Populism flourished. Eventually the movement founded a People's Party. Farmers often saw themselves as the true American people. As such, they were resentful that a new urbanized society and new economic groups often profited at the expense of farmers. Railroad owners and bankers were among the worst offenders against farmers' welfare. While populists failed to elect their own presidential candidate, the populist goal of greater government regulation was realized in a later period.

Defining Populism

🔊 Vocabulary Book

The issues that were important to populist supporters are not always readily understood today, especially those that concern the money supply. Have students create a Vocabulary Book of ten terms or popular nouns on populism: *greenback, inflation, deflation, Grange, cooperative, People's Party, William Jennings Bryan, graduated income tax, silverite, goldbug.*

Materials Needed: one sheet of 8.5" by 11" paper, scissors.

Analyzing Political Platforms

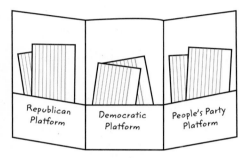

🔊 Three-Pocket Book

The political challenges of the 1890s made for a dynamic situation among the parties, especially with the challenge of a third party, the Populist Party. Have students create a Foldable to help them analyze the platforms of the three parties. Different students might organize the parties' platforms according to the problems the electorate perceived, or according to the groups and/or regions each party appealed to.

Materials Needed: one sheet of 8.5" by 17" paper, glue, index cards.

Cause and Effect: The Populist Movement

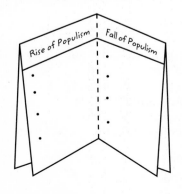

⬅ Folded Book

Students will be able to understand the rise and fall of populism by making this Foldable. Students should review their text or other material on populism, being sure to take note of the factors behind its rise, and factors behind its decline. They should then list both sets of factors in a Folded Book Foldable.

Materials Needed: one sheet of 8.5" by 11" paper.

Imperialism: Becoming a World Power

TOPIC SUMMARY

It was the Industrial Revolution that made nations into imperialist powers. A nation with a strong industrial economy needed world markets. Controlling regions overseas helped guarantee those markets. Nations in Western Europe blazed the imperialist trail, but the United States followed the European path after its industrial power was established. The annexation of the Philippines after the Spanish-American War sent a strong signal to other nations that the United States was ready to compete on the world scene.

Summarizing the Forces of Imperialism

Territory	Reasons for Acquisition	Results of Acquisition
Alaska		
Hawaii		
Philippines		

🎧 Folded Table

Imperialism is a complex phenomenon. It developed from a number of motives. It involved government as well as business and other groups in society. It also concerned different parts of the world, and European competitors. Have students create a Folded Table to summarize some of this information, aligning areas acquired with the reasons for and results of that American acquisition.

Materials Needed: one sheet of 8.5" by 11" paper.

Compare and Contrast

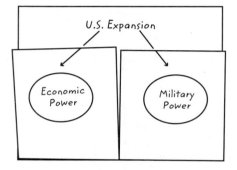

🎧 Concept-Map Book

By creating this Foldable, students can understand the relationship between economic and military power, as well as how both reflect imperialism. Have students review the material, reflecting on how and whether growth in the economy and the military are related. They should be careful especially to note the years in which both developments occurred. Events or developments will be listed under the military power tab and the economic power tab.

Materials Needed: one sheet of 8.5" by 11" paper.

Identifying Provisions of the Platt Amendment

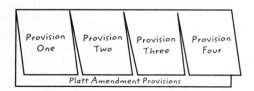

◖ Four-Tab Book

While the United States did not annex Cuba outright, it nevertheless established strong control over that Caribbean nation. The means of control are well laid out in the Platt Amendment. This is an important piece of legislation for students to understand because it highlights how American imperialism sometimes operated in Latin America.

Materials Needed: one 8.5" by 11" sheet of paper, scissors.

The Progressives

TOPIC SUMMARY

The Progressive era is one of the most important periods in modern American history. Progressive reformers were responding to a new industrial, urbanized society that threatened to overwhelm existing institutions. Initially city governments responded to these pressures, especially the pressure of a growing immigrant population, with the political machine. Political corruption followed, however, and the Progressive campaign began. A rational and social scientific approach underlay the ideas of most Progressives. Their pioneering reforms set a model for modern reform, notably the New Deal.

Tracing Progressive Influence

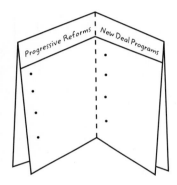

◖ Folded Chart

Students can trace the lasting significance of Progressive reforms by creating this Foldable. The Foldable is best utilized after students have studied New Deal programs. Have students create a two-column Folded Chart, listing specific reforms in the first column, and a related or similar political or social reform passed during the Great Depression of the 1930s. Students should include dates in their lists, and enough description to see the link.

Materials Needed: one sheet of 8.5" by 11" paper.

Analyzing Reform Programs

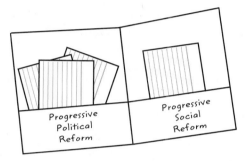

◖ Pocket Book

The Progressive agenda was divided into political reforms and social reforms. Students can understand the nature of the difference between the two by working on this Foldable. Students should take notes on a wide range of reforms, placing each one in the proper column of the Foldable.

Materials Needed: one sheet of 8.5" by 11" paper, glue, index cards.

Summarizing Progressivism

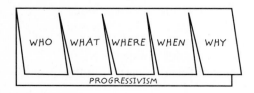

◖ Five-Tab Book

Students can create a handy study review guide by creating this Foldable. Students should take notes on basic facts about the movement, then label the five tabs with the heading of Who, What, Where, When, and Why. When they list the relevant facts under each tab, they should be specific. For example, under Where, they would list the major urban centers where Progressivism was strong, or give brief biographical information for reformers under Who.

Materials Needed: one sheet of 8.5" by 11" paper.

The Progressive Spirit and the Presidency

TOPIC SUMMARY

Teddy Roosevelt's administration from 1901 to 1909 introduced a new model for the American presidency. Before taking office, Roosevelt had taken a leading role in Progressive reforms in the state of New York. That, and the fact of his own ebullient personality, led him to take an activist and optimistic view of the government role in American life. The administrations of William Taft and Woodrow Wilson also reflected the ideas of Progressivism.

Compare and Contrast

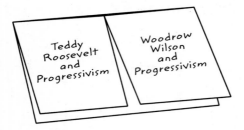

🔒 Two-Tab Book

Students will be able to sharpen their understanding of Progressivism by making this Foldable. After they have studied the presidencies of both Theodore Roosevelt and Woodrow Wilson, students should create a Two-Tab Book with information on the Progressive aspects of their administrations. The information should include a brief description of each man's views on the role of government, and a short list of his Progressive policies.

Materials Needed: one sheet of 8.5" by 11" paper, scissors.

Categorizing Progressive Presidents

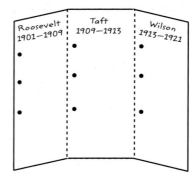

🔒 Trifold Book

Three presidents can be said to represent the Progressive era. Have students create a Trifold Book to aid in their study of how Progressivism changed during the administrations of Theodore Roosevelt, William Taft, and Woodrow Wilson. For each administration, students can list: the dates of each man's presidency, the domestic issues, the foreign issues, and any Progressive accomplishments.

Materials Needed: one sheet of 11" by 17" paper.

Summarizing Progressivism's Impact

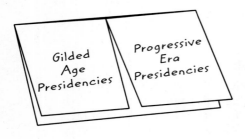

Materials Needed: one sheet of 11" by 17" paper.

🔒 Two-Tab Book

Have students create a Two-Tab Book with labels of *Gilded Age Presidencies* and *Progressive Era Presidencies*. Students should name the Presidents of the Gilded Age, roughly from 1877 to 1896, and describe their political, economic, and social policies. These can be contrasted with political, economic, and social policies of Presidents during the Progressive era.

World War I

TOPIC SUMMARY

Because of its large economy, the United States came of age as a world power during the presidency of Theodore Roosevelt. Yet when World War I began, the nation was reluctant to become involved in world affairs. German interference in the New World eventually triggered American entry into the war. Experience with the Versailles Peace Treaty negotiations, especially the request for American participation in the League of Nations, however, returned to a spirit of isolationism.

Categorizing Allied and Central Powers

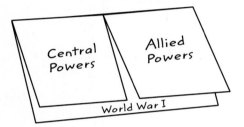

🔊 Two-Tab Book

Have students create a Two-Tab Foldable that reports briefly on the countries which made up the Allied and Central powers in World War I. Under the tab, students should list the following: each country in the alliance; and why it joined the alliance or what reasons it had for opposing countries in the opposing alliance.

Materials Needed: one sheet of 8.5" by 11" paper, scissors.

Sequencing World War I Events

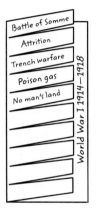

🔊 Vocabulary Book

Students can create a Foldable that serves as a reminder of the events and conditions of World War I. On their ten-tab Vocabulary Book, they might consider defining the following: *Battle of the Somme, attrition, trench warfare, poison gas, no man's land, doughboy, Treaty of Brest-Litovsk.*

Materials Needed: one sheet of 8.5" by 11" paper, scissors.

Analyzing the Peace

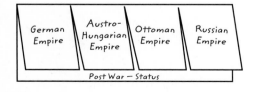

◖ Four-Tab Book

By creating a Four-Tab Book, students can create a Foldable study reference on the impact of World War I. On each tab, students should list: German Empire, Austro-Hungarian Empire, Ottoman Empire, Russian Empire. Under each tab, the students should describe the outcome of the war in that country, including changes in government or borders.

Materials Needed: one sheet of 8.5" by 11" paper, scissors.

Women's Suffrage

TOPIC SUMMARY

In 1920, women obtained the right to vote when the Nineteenth Amendment to the Constitution was ratified. Women's suffrage came when it did in part because of World War I—many women had proved the caliber of their citizenship during the war. Yet the way had been paved over decades of campaigning by leading suffragists beginning with Susan B. Anthony and Lucretia Mott in the 1840s. The first women's rights convention was held in Seneca, New York, in 1848.

Compare and Contrast Suffrage Movements

SUFFRAGE MOVEMENTS	Women	African American
Date Campaigns Begin		
Supporting Arguments		
Events Inspiring Passage		
Date of Suffrage		

🔂 Folded Chart

African Americans and women achieved suffrage at different times. It is also true that formal passage of suffrage did not always result immediately result in actual implementation of suffrage. Have students create a Folded Chart of two columns in order to list pertinent facts about the campaign for and winning of suffrage. Facts noted might include: the dates of early campaigns for suffrage; the arguments presented; events that prompted Congressional legislation and its name; when suffrage was actually implemented and why.

Materials Needed: one sheet of 8.5" by 11" paper.

Explaining Suffragist Motives

🔂 Bound Book

To acquire a more personal understanding of suffragists, students can create a Bound Book Foldable on a suffragist of their choice. They may choose a woman named in the text or found in further research. After learning something about the life of their figure, students should write several brief entries reflecting the inner thoughts of a suffragist at a critical point in the suffrage movement.

Materials Needed: two sheets of 8.5" by 11" paper, scissors.

Sequencing the Women's Suffrage Movement

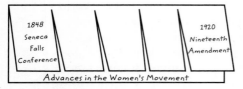

🔄 Five-Tab Book

Students should review the highlights of the women's suffrage movement from the 1840s through 1920. They should then select five events or notable developments to place on an annotated time line in a Five-Tab Foldable. The students' notes on each entry should suggest why the development was significant in the history of women.

Materials Needed: one sheet of 8.5" by 11" paper, scissors.

Jazz Age

TOPIC SUMMARY

The Jazz Age, or the "Roaring Twenties," was filled with cultural and social change. Often, it was the younger generation who promoted change. Disillusioned by the war, many set out to express their freedom from older values. This feeling was visible in the dress of the "flapper," but also in music, art, and literature. The Harlem Renaissance among African Americans is one important part of Jazz Age changes. All these cultural changes made rural and small town Americans uncomfortable. They saw the freer lifestyle as immoral and their resistance was expressed in the Prohibition movement, in religious fundamentalism, and in a Ku Klux Klan revival.

Categorizing the Harlem Renaissance

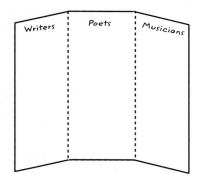

🔓 Trifold Book

Have students create a Trifold Book to present a brief biography, with artistic works, of major figures in the Harlem Renaissance under the category of writers, poets, and musicians. Students may want to expand on their entries by searching on the Internet.

Materials Needed: one sheet of 8.5" by 11" paper.

Explaining the Scopes Trial

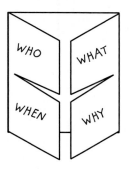

🔓 Four-Door Book

Students can make their understanding of 1920s fundamentalism more concrete by creating a Foldable on the 1925 Scopes trial. In a Four-Door Book, students should use the labels of *Who, What, When* and *Why* to list as many explanatory facts as possible on the Scopes trial. For example, under *Who*, students would list important people involved, such as the defendant, the defense counsel, and the prosecutor, with brief identifications.

Materials Needed: one sheet of 11" by 17" paper, scissors.

Describing the Clash of Cultures

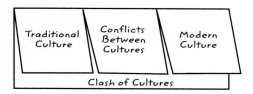

🔓 Three-Tab Book

Students should be introduced to the overall theme of the clash between the older, bourgeois culture and Jazz Age values. They should take notes with this focus as they read the text. They will then be able to creating a Three-Tab Foldable. Characteristics of the traditional culture (for example, work and duty) and of the modern culture can be listed under the two outer tabs. Events and developments that reflect this clash should be under the middle tab.

Materials Needed: one sheet of 8.5" by 11" paper, scissors.

Postwar Economic Boom

TOPIC SUMMARY

A famous saying sums up an important part of American life: "The business of America is business." The saying was very apt for the 1920s. The nation's resources were directed toward mass production and consumption. Prosperity brought new goods and services to an expanding middle class. It also promoted new forms of popular entertainment—radio, movies, jazz, magazines, and spectator sports like baseball. Such popular entertainment was designed to appeal to the average man and woman and to make money. The commercialized entertainment world that is still with us today originated in this period.

Defining 1920s Prosperity

🔻 Vocabulary Book Foldable

In the 1920s, government's economic policies reflected a belief in business principles, especially as promoted by Secretary of the Treasurer Andrew Mellon. Students can enhance their understanding of these economic policies by creating a Vocabulary Book of ten terms. Students might include terms such as the following: *mass production, assembly line, welfare capitalism, open shop, Model T, Andrew Mellon, supply-side economics, cooperative individualism, moratorium, isolationism.* Students can write their definition inside under the appropriate tab.

Materials Needed: one sheet of notebook paper, scissors.

Analyzing the Roaring Twenties

Impact on Society	In the 1920s	Today
Automobiles		
Buying on Credit		
Motion Pictures		

🔻 Folded Chart Foldable

Ask students to use a Folded Chart to describe the impact of automobiles, credit, and movies on American society. First have students list the ways in which those innovations affected people's lives in the 1920s. Then have students list the ways in which those things affect Americans today.

Materials Needed: one sheet of 11" x 17" paper.

Comparing and Contrasting Presidents

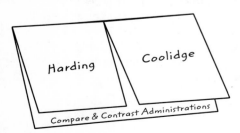

◖ Two-Tab Book Foldable

Ask students to research the Harding and Coolidge administrations and record their findings in a Two-Tab Foldable. Encourage students to describe how the two presidents and their ways of governing were similar and how they were different.

Materials Needed: one sheet of 8.5" x 11" paper, scissors.

The Great Depression

TOPIC SUMMARY

October 1929 is infamous for the crash of the New York Stock Exchange and the beginning of the Great Depression. Panic selling of stock, with little willingness to buy, drastically reduced the value of shares. The crash wiped out people's investments, business capital, and banks' cash reserves. Reduced business activity put many people out of work, and widened the gap between rich and poor. Millions of Americans lived in poverty, further reducing their ability to buy goods and services. As trade declined, the depression spread worldwide.

Analyzing Popular Culture

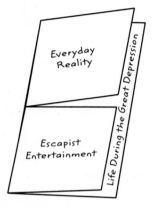

⬆ Two-Tab Book

Ask students to research the way people coped with adversity during the Depression. Have students read about popular entertainment of the 1930s, such as movies and radio. Students should use a in a Two-Tab Foldable to list examples of the hardships people endured in real life and the kinds of entertainment that flourished.

Materials Needed: one sheet of 8.5" x 11" paper, scissors.

Interpreting Actions and Results

Hoover's Actions	Description	Result
Public Works		
Agricultural Marking Act		
Reconstruction Finance Corp.		
Emergency Relief Act		

⬆ Folded Chart Foldable

Have students use a Folded Chart to assess the effectiveness of President Hoover's policies in response to the Great Depression. First ask students to describe measures the government took, then have them describe the results of those measures.

Materials Needed: one sheet of 11" x 17" paper.

Comparing Economic Stability

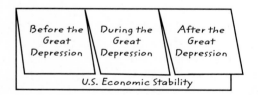

⬅ Three-Tab Book

Ask students to assess the stability of the United States economy before, during, and after the Great Depression based on their reading. Have students compare the three periods in terms of unemployment, the stock market, productivity, and growth. Students should list their assessments in a Three-Tab Foldable.

Materials Needed: one sheet of 8.5" x 11" paper, scissors.

The New Deal

TOPIC SUMMARY

Beginning with the sweeping legislation of the Hundred Days, Franklin Roosevelt's presidency remade the way the U.S. government solves problems. Roosevelt's New Deal programs aggressively sought to ensure the welfare of citizens by creating jobs, building public projects, and providing relief to the needy. Roosevelt personally sought to reassure and inspire the public that the nation would succeed in pulling out of the Depression.

Defining Key Terms

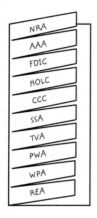

ⓕ Vocabulary Book Foldable

Have students list the following terms on the outside tabs of a Ten-Tab Foldable: *NRA, AAA, FDIC, HOLC, CCC, SSA, TVA, PWA, WPA, REA.* Then ask students to find each term in the text, write out what the initials stand for on the inside of the booklet, and describe the function of the government agency or program.

Materials Needed: one sheet of notebook paper, scissors.

Analyzing Long-Term Effects

New Deal Measures	Purpose in the 1930s	Effects Today
Social Security		
National Labor Relations Board		
Federal Deposit Insurance Corp.		

ⓕ Folded Chart Foldable

Ask students to construct a Folded Chart showing selected New Deal programs and their long-term consequences. In one column of the Folded Chart, students can describe in a phrase or two a program's original purpose. In the second column, students should identify briefly how those changes influence government and society today.

Materials Needed: one sheet of 11" x 17" paper.

Profiling Eleanor Roosevelt

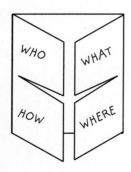

ⓒ Four-Door Book Foldable

Ask students to compile facts about the life and work of Eleanor Roosevelt. Have students research who she was, what she did, where she came from, and how she helped change American society. Then have students report their findings in a Four-Door Foldable. Encourage them to be as specific as possible.

Materials Needed: one sheet of 8.5" x 11" paper, scissors.

World War II

TOPIC SUMMARY

World War II devastated much of Europe and Asia, as the Allies, including Britain, France, the U.S. and the Soviet Union, fought to stop the expansionist Axis powers of Germany, Italy, and Japan. Initially providing only aid to Britain, an isolationist American public was finally drawn into the war with the Japanese attack at Pearl Harbor. The nation mobilized its military and industrial resources to wage war in Europe and the Pacific, achieving victory and world leadership.

Comparing Totalitarian Dictators

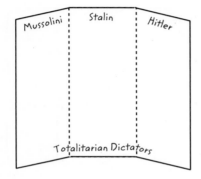

Trifold Book

Ask students to construct a Trifold Foldable to compare and contrast the dictatorships of Benito Mussolini, Josef Stalin, and Adolf Hitler. Have students use the Foldable to list facts about each ruler under his name. This will be a helpful study guide on their differences and similarities in the totalitarian systems of the three men.

Materials Needed: one sheet of 8.5 x 11" paper.

Creating a Time Line

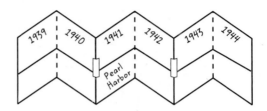

Accordion Book Foldable

Ask students to make a World War II time line spanning the years 1939-1945. Have students select major events to include, such as the U.S. entry into the war. They may choose to focus on military battles, or they may want to plot diplomatic and political events like the Nazi-Soviet Non-Aggression pact. Students should use the Accordion Foldable, using four sheets in order to have 7 sections to cover the time period—the last section can be cut off.

Materials Needed: four sheets of 8.5" x 11" paper, scissors, glue.

Analyzing the Holocaust

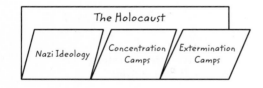

Concept-Map Book

Ask students to compile facts about the Holocaust and present them in a Concept-Map Foldable. Have students organize their information into three categories: the reasoning behind the Holocaust, according to Nazi ideology; the establishment of concentration camps; and the "final solution" of extermination camps.

Materials Needed: one sheet of 8.5" x 11" paper, scissors.

World War II: The Home Front

TOPIC SUMMARY

As with the previous world war, World War II was a total war involving all of civil society, not just the military. Every citizen was viewed as part of the war effort—women worked in factories, families planted victory gardens, young children participated in scrap metal drives, and men not at the front devoted their spare hours to civil defense. Efforts on the home front sometimes had lasting effects. Women, for example, would not forget their opportunity to work in jobs usually reserved for men.

Summarizing American Life During World War II

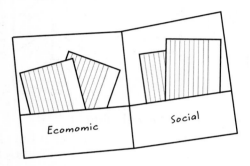

◐ Pocket Book

Students may use a Pocket Book to help them summarize the various aspects of daily life that World War II affected. Have them create this Foldable, labeling the two pockets as *Economic, Social.* For economic effects, students would include not only general effects on prosperity, but specific economic programs that dealt with aspects of the economy, such as the Office of Price Administration. The same general rule would apply to social effects.

Materials Needed: one sheet of 8.5" by 11" paper, glue.

Interpreting Social Change

INFLUENCE OF WWII	Pre-War Status	Postwar Status	Assess Change
Women			
African Americans			

◐ Folded Chart

By creating this Foldable, students can create a visual review of the social changes stemming from World War II. Have them create a Folded Chart with four columns: INFLUENCE OF WWII, Pre-War Status, Postwar Status, and Assess Change. Under INFLUENCE OF WWII, list Women and African Americans. Then describe the social and economic position of women and African Americans in columns 2 and 3; in the last column, students should write a brief statement on what had and had not changed.

Materials Needed: one sheet of 8.5" by 11" paper.

Interpreting the Japanese American Experience

A Day in an Internment Camp

◑ Bound Book

Students can create a Foldable to contain their creative interpretation of some Japanese Americans' lives during World War II. After they have read the textbook on the topic—and perhaps conducted Internet research as well—they can write entries for different times of day to represent "A Day in an Internment Camp." Students may wish to write them from the point -of-view of someone their own age.

Materials Needed: two sheets of 8.5" by 11" paper, scissors.

The Cold War

TOPIC SUMMARY

The Cold War began with the end of World War II. The roots of the conflict can be traced to the fact that the Soviet system was diametrically opposed to the democratic and capitalist governments of the West. The initial disputes were over the fate of Eastern European nations, where the Soviets demanded control. For almost 50 years, the war continued as the Soviets' attempted to strengthen and expand communism while the United States directed its foreign policy at containing that expansion.

Analyzing Democracy and Communism

COLD WAR CONTRASTS	Political Differences	Economic Differences
United States		
Soviet Union		

🔼 Folded Table

Students can create a Foldable to represent the important differences between the world's two superpowers between roughly 1945 and 1991. Students should focus their text review on the political and economic systems of the United States and the Soviet Union at that period. In a Folded Table, they can list specific characteristics of those systems for each nation.

Materials Needed: one sheet of 8.5" by 11" paper.

Distinguishing Causes

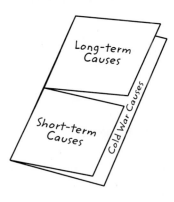

🔼 Two-Tab Book

Encourage students to review their textbook to find long-term and short-term causes of the Cold War. For example, remind them that a long-term cause would include an event such as American intervention in the Russian Civil War of 1918–1921, while a short-term cause would include the dispute over Poland at the Yalta Conference.

Materials Needed: one sheet of 8.5" by 11" paper.

Sequencing Cold War Effects

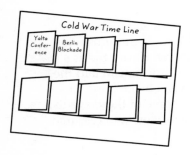

◖ Billboard Project

Students can make this Foldable in order to have an annotated time line for reviewing major events of the Cold War. On each billboard section, a significant event of the Cold War era can be named—for example, the Berlin crisis, the founding of NATO and the Warsaw Pact, the Korean War, and the Cuban missile crisis. Inside each section, students can write a short bulleted list with a) the date of the event; b) a brief description of it; and c) its significance for U.S.-Soviet relations.

Materials Needed: poster board, four or five half-sheets of 8.5" x 11" paper, glue.

McCarthyism

TOPIC SUMMARY

In the early 1950s, Cold War fears were intense because of the possibility of a nuclear war. In 1950, Wisconsin Senator Joseph McCarthy began exploiting these fears by accusing government officials of being Communist spies. Anyone associated with his targets was also suspect. Despite his rashness and lack of solid evidence, McCarthy was able for awhile to convince many citizens that the government was riddled with enemies. First Amendments rights were endangered during this period, but in 1954, Congress censored McCarthy for his unconstitutional tactics.

Summarizing McCarthyism

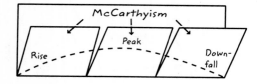

🎧 Concept-Map Book

Using a Concept-Map Foldable, students can summarize the course of the McCarthy "Red Scare." Students should use the foldable to identify the stages of McCarthyism—its rise, peak and downfall. Underneath each heading, students should briefly identify the causes for each stage.

Materials Needed: one sheet of 8.5" by 11" paper.

Analyzing Political Movements

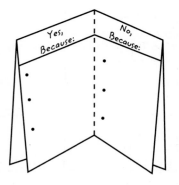

🎧 Half Book

Students can enhance their understanding of the general significance of McCarthyism by creating this Foldable. Have them work on a Half Book Foldable that addresses the question: "Could a McCarthyism movement arise today?" Inside, students should complete the Foldable by answering "Yes" and why, or "No" and why.

Materials Needed: one sheet of 8.5" by 11" paper.

Identifying Precursors to McCarthyism

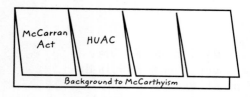

🄲 Four-Tab Book

Even before McCarthyism developed, certain events showed a strong fear of communism in the United States. Students can clarify their understanding of how anticommunism laid the groundwork for McCarthyism by creating this Foldable. Have students make a Four-Tab Book to list and briefly identify some of these events, such the McCarran Act or HUAC. Some students may want to take a longer view and research events since 1917 that contributed to American anticommunism.

Materials Needed: one sheet of 8.5" by 11" paper.

The Affluent Society

TOPIC SUMMARY

The post-World War II economy introduced a new prosperity for many Americans. The middle class grew. More people owned homes in the suburbs, and more people had expendable income. In his well-known book, economist John Kenneth Galbraith introduced the term *affluent society,* referring to the seemingly infinite variety of goods and services Americans could now buy. Many Americans did not share in the prosperity, however. Greater prosperity soon led some leaders to suggest that the government should do more to help those people unable to achieve "the good life."

Defining the Affluent Society

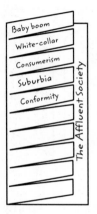

🎧 Vocabulary Book

Have students create their own list of 10 review terms for the affluent society of the 1950s by reviewing their text. Terms might include: *white-collar, baby boom, consumerism, postwar economic boom, suburbia, Levittown,* and *conformity.* Music and book titles could also be included.

Materials Needed: one sheet of 8.5" by 11" paper.

Compare and Contrast

Popular Culture	1950s	Present
Mass Media Types		
Youth Culture		
Groups Represented in Media		

🎧 Folded Table

By creating a Folded Table on popular culture in the 1950s and the present, students will be able to think about some of the differences between the two eras, such as the issues of interest to young people, or how commercialized popular culture is now compared to then. Have students list the following for both time periods: data on the types of mass media and size of the audiences for them; characteristics of youth culture; groups represented in the mass media.

Materials Needed: one sheet of 8.5" by 11" paper.

Analyzing the Postwar Baby Boom

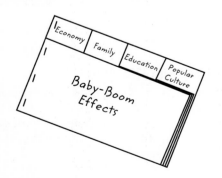

◖ Top-Tab Book

Students should review any relevant chapter material for the baby-boom of the 1950s and 1960s and then create the Top-Tab Foldable. The various tabs of the Foldable allows students to briefly explain the effects of the baby boom on various aspects of society—the economy, the family, education, and popular culture.

Materials Needed: three sheets of 8.5" by 11" paper.

Johnson and the Great Society

TOPIC SUMMARY

American idealism and a prosperous society inspired support for President Lyndon Johnson's Great Society programs. Johnson wanted to reduce poverty among certain groups in the nation. Federal funds were targeted at programs for poor people in the inner cities and in rural areas, such as Appalachia. In Johnson's vision, education was a key to more citizens achieving a higher quality of life—the American dream. While the short-lived program fell short of its goals, it introduced models for a number of programs that still exist in American society, such as in-home services for the elderly, day care, and job training.

Analyzing Causes for the Great Society

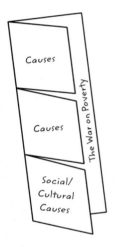

🕮 Three-Tab Book

Students should consider the causes that contributed to the creation of, and support for, the Great Society programs of the 1960s. They should reflect these causes by type in a Three-Tab Foldable under economic causes, political causes, and social/cultural causes. Students should be as specific as possible in their language.

Materials Needed: one sheet of 8.5" by 11" paper, scissors.

Categorizing Great Society Programs

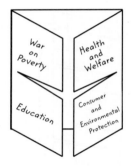

🕮 Four-Door Book

Multiple initiatives made up President Johnson's Great Society agenda. Students can create a handy study guide for this complex government program by creating this Foldable. Have them make a Four-Door Book with major headings on the front of the "doors." Specific programs can be listed inside for four major categories: Health and Welfare, the War on Poverty, Education, Consumer and Environmental Protection.

Materials Needed: one 11" by 17" sheet of paper.

Compare and Contrast

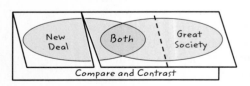

🕮 Three-Tab Book With Venn Diagram

Student can sharpen their understanding of the Great Society, as well as of the New Deal, by creating this Foldable. Have them create a Three-Tab Book that will serve as a comparison of goals and programs of the New Deal and Great Society. Shared characteristics and programs will be listed under the center tab of the Three-Tab Book.

Materials Needed: one sheet of 8.5" by 11" paper, scissors.

The Civil Rights Movement

TOPIC SUMMARY

The idealism of the Kennedy and Johnson era was most evident in the civil rights movement. Although both presidents provided support for it, the modern civil rights movement was a grass-roots movement which can be traced back to World War II. Martin Luther King, Jr., led the campaign to achieve political equality with whites. His inspirational leadership of nonviolent protest inspired white Americans. Success was assured when President Lyndon Johnson committed his notable political talents to passing the milestone voting rights legislation of 1964 and 1965.

Sequencing Civil Rights Events

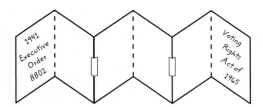

🎧 Accordion Book

Students can create a civil rights time line with an Accordion Book Foldable. They can use as many sheets as needed to fit their number of entries. Have students review material on civil rights during the World War II period, as well as the movement that gathered force after the *Brown* v. *Board of Education* decision. They can then select important events for roughly 20 years of civil rights history, beginning with Roosevelt's Executive Order 8802 of June, 1941. The time line should include brief notes on each event.

Materials Needed: three or more sheets of 8.5" by 11" paper, scissors, glue.

Compare and Contrast Civil Rights Eras

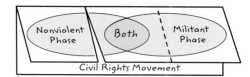

🎧 Three-Tab Book With Venn Diagram

Students can create a Three-Tab Book in order to highlight the differences between two stages of the civil rights movement: the early, largely nonviolent stage led by Martin Luther King, Jr., and the later militant stage led by men like Stokely Carmichael and Malcolm X. For each stage, students might describe a) the goals; b) the methods of their campaign; and c) social groups and organizations in support. Common elements would be listed under "Both."

Materials Needed: one sheet of 8.5" by 11" paper, scissors.

Defining the Civil Rights Movement

⟲ Vocabulary Book

Between the Supreme Court's *Brown* v. *Board of Education* decision (1954) and passage of the Civil Rights Act in 1964, many issues and events marked the advance of civil rights for African Americans. Have students review the text to gather terms related to these important developments. They can then create a civil rights lexicon of ten terms. They can choose their own terms, but some examples include: *Gandhi, Thurgood Marshall, "separate but equal," Montgomery bus boycott, nonviolent protest, sit-in.*

Materials Needed: one sheet of 8.5" by 11" paper, scissors.

The Vietnam War

TOPIC SUMMARY

United States involvement in Vietnam began as an attempt to contain the communist regime of North Vietnam and preserve the non-communist regime of South Vietnam. The U.S. commitment began with a few military advisers in the late 1950s, but by the war's end, about 58,000 Americans had lost their lives in the fighting. More than 2 million Vietnamese died. The war divided public opinion, arousing a protest movement during the 1960s that permanently altered American society.

Chronicling Phases of the War

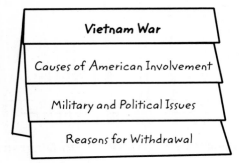

◑ Layered-Look Book

Students should create a Layered-Look Book to chronicle the Vietnam War. After reviewing information on the war, students should organize the information into three categories: causes of American involvement; military and political issues that arose during the war; the reasons for American withdrawal. Encourage students to include political, military, economic, and diplomatic dimensions of American involvement.

Materials Needed: two sheets of 8.5" x 11" paper, stapler.

Defining Vietnam Terminology

◑ Vocabulary Book

Ask students to create a Foldable that will aid their review study of the Vietnam War. They should select terms as they read the chapter and then create a 10-tab Vocabulary Book. Students will choose different terms, but examples might include *Ho Chi Minh, containment, domino theory, guerrilla warfare, Dien Bien Phu, Geneva Accords, Vietminh,* and the *Gulf of Tonkin* resolution. Terms will be defined under each tab as appropriate.

Materials Needed: one sheet of 8.5" x 11" paper, scissors.

Clarifying Opposing Arguments

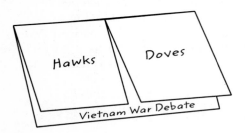

◖ Two-Tab Book

Ask students to research the reasons people gave for and against U.S. foreign policy during the war in Vietnam. Students can then list the major arguments in a Two-Tab Foldable under the headings *Hawks* and *Doves*.

Materials Needed: one sheet of 8.5" x 11" paper, scissors.

Voices of Protest

TOPIC SUMMARY

Protest took many forms and concerned many issues in the later twentieth century. Students demanded more control over their education. Antiwar activists opposed U.S. foreign policy and resisted the draft. Women and minority groups pressed for equal rights in employment, education, housing, and public service. Environmentalists fought pollution and over-consumption of resources. Social justice movements influenced popular music, clothing styles, the arts, and the media.

Organizing Information

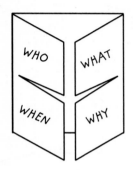

Four-Door Book

Have students choose an event, such as the Berkeley Free Speech Movement, Earth Day, the Woodstock Music Festival, Students for a Democratic Society (SDS), or the National Organization for Women (NOW) to report on. Students can organize their information in a Four-Door Foldable, answering the questions, who, what, when, and why.

Materials Needed: one sheet of 8.5" x 11" paper, scissors.

Researching Discrimination

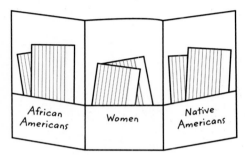

Three-Pocket Book

Have students review their text on three disadvantaged groups that organized to fight discrimination: African Americans, Hispanic Americans, or Native Americans. Students record key facts about their goals and campaigns for change on 3" by 5" note cards and place them in a Three-Pocket Foldable.

Materials Needed: 3" x 5" note cards, one sheet of 11" x 17" paper, glue.

Comparing Politics and Culture

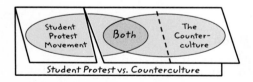

Three-Tab Book With Venn Diagram

Ask students to compile facts about two separate, though related movements of the 1960s and early 1970s: the student protest movement and the counterculture. Students should note similarities and differences between the ideas, people, and events in the two movements. Have them record their findings in a Three-Tab Foldable, with common characteristics in the overlapping circle.

Materials Needed: one sheet of 8.5" x 11" paper, scissors.

Nixon and Watergate

TOPIC SUMMARY

After winning a close election in 1968, Richard Nixon solidified Republican control of the presidency with a landslide victory in 1972. President Nixon made historic moves in foreign policy and built a coalition of conservatives from all regions of the country. When he faced probable impeachment and conviction on charges stemming from the Watergate scandal, however, he resigned the presidency.

Evaluating the Nixon Presidency

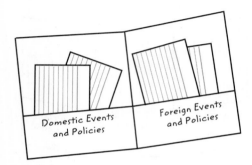

🏛 Pocket Book

Ask students to find four or more examples of events and policies during the Nixon presidency. Students should take notes on 3" x 5" cards as they review material in their textbook, separating their findings into foreign and domestic categories. Have students organize their note cards in a Two-Pocket Foldable. The Foldable can then be used as a reference in assessing the strengths and weaknesses of the Nixon administration.

Materials Needed: 3" x 5" note cards, one sheet of 8.5" x 11" paper, glue.

Analyzing Cause and Effect

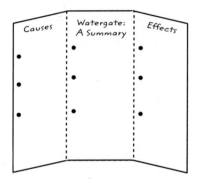

🏛 Shutter Fold

After students have read about the Watergate scandal, they can create a Shutter Fold to analyze critical information on this event. Students can write a brief summary of Watergate events in the large middle section inside the Shutter Foldable. One the left-hand tab, they can list the causes of the Watergate scandal; on the right-hand tab, they should list the effects of Watergate on the political system.

Materials Needed: one sheet of 11" x 17" paper, scissors.

Creating a Watergate Time Line

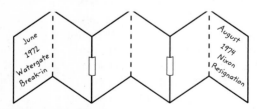

☚ Accordion Book

By creating a time line, students can better understand how the illegal and subversive activities of the Nixon administration were uncovered and how they led to his impeachment. Using the Accordion book, students can trace how the Watergate scandal unfolded, beginning with the break-in of Democratic Party headquarters at the Watergate Hotel in June 1972, and ending with Nixon's resignation on August 1974.

Materials Needed: three sheets of 8.5" by 11" paper, scissors, glue.

Reagan and the New Conservatism

TOPIC SUMMARY

In the 1980s, there was a resurgence of conservatism, as mainstream society reacted to the social upheavals of the 1960s and 1970s. Republican Ronald Reagan was elected President in 1980. For some, he symbolized the simplicity, confidence and traditional religious values of an older America. The 1980s was also a period of economic growth, tax cuts, and cuts in social welfare spending. Because Reagan also spent huge amounts on a military build-up, however, the government budget deficit had climbed to about $200 billion by the time he left office.

Chronicling Major Events

🎧 Layered-Look Book

Have students research the foreign policy record of Presidents Ronald Reagan. Ask students to focus on policies for different countries discussed in their textbook, such as Iran, Central America, and the Soviet Union. Students should summarize their findings in a Layered Foldable, briefly describing the policy for each nation and describing its impact.

Materials Needed: two sheets of 8.5" x 11" paper, stapler.

Analyzing the Reagan Revolution

The Reagan Revolution	Before Reagan	Reagan Era	After Reagan
Domestic Policy			
Foreign Policy			

🎧 Folded Chart

Ask students to create a Folded Chart to reflect the changes in American government under President Ronald Reagan. The students' Foldables should list domestic and foreign policy for three eras: the decade or so before the Reagan era, the Reagan administration, and the post-Reagan years.

Materials Needed: one sheet of 11" x 17" paper.

Identifying Ideologies

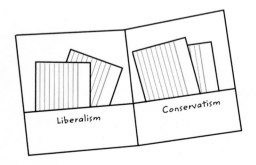

🌒 Two-Pocket Book

Students can come to a quicker understanding of political ideology by creating this Foldable. Have students take notes on the ideas and values of liberalism and conservatism. Students should be as specific as possible, giving examples that relate to different areas of life, that is, the political, the economic, and the social. These characteristics can be listed on 3" x 5" cards and organized in a Three-Pocket Foldable.

Materials Needed: 3" x 5" note cards, one sheet of 11" x 17" paper, glue.

The New Century

TOPIC SUMMARY

Technology has introduced new developments and challenges in the United States. Computer technology has dramatically affected the economy and daily life. The effects of Internet technology have also been dramatic, creating a global economy and cultural diffusion. It is not certain whether increased global trade will benefit all nations equally in the longer run. A second development of the late 20th and early 21st century is an unwelcome one: an increasing incidence of terrorism both at home and abroad.

Surveying Technological Changes

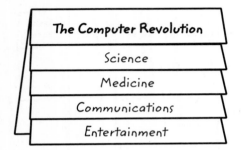

The Computer Revolution
Science
Medicine
Communications
Entertainment

🎧 Layered-Look Book

Have students research the impact of computers on American life. Ask students to consider such fields as business, scientific research, medical treatment and diagnosis, communications, and entertainment. Have students summarize their findings in a Layered Foldable, briefly describing computer applications in each field and how they have changed the way people live.

Materials Needed: two sheets of 8.5" x 11" paper, stapler.

Defining Key Terms

Standard of living
NAFTA
Trade deficit
Balance of trade
Global economy

🎧 Vocabulary Book

Students can create a Vocabulary to reinforce their understanding of economic issues in the 21st century. Students can create their own list by reviewing the text and/or by supplementing their research on the Internet. Terms might include: *standard of living, NAFTA, trade deficit, balance of trade, global economy, euro, World Trade Organization, telecommute, "dot.com economy," APEC (Asia Pacific Economic Cooperation)*.

Materials Needed: one sheet of notebook paper, scissors.

Reporting the War on Terrorism

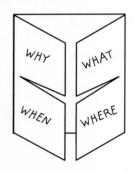

WHY | WHAT
WHEN | WHERE

⟲ Four-Door Book

Ask students to compile facts about the terrorist attacks at the World Trade Center and Pentagon on September 11, 2001. From the text information, students should answer the questions what, when, where, and why about these events. This information should be recorded in a Four-Door Foldable.

Materials Needed: one sheet of 8.5" x 11" paper, scissors.